WE
CAN ALL
GET ALONG

50 Steps You Can Take
to Help End Racism

FOR YOURSELF • FOR YOUR FAMILY
• FOR YOUR COMMUNITY •
FOR THE NATION • FOR THE WORLD

Clyde W. Ford

A DELL TRADE PAPERBACK

A DELL TRADE PAPERBACK

Published by
Dell Publishing
a division of
Bantam Doubleday Dell Publishing Group, Inc.
1540 Broadway
New York, New York 10036

Please note organizations, addresses, and phone numbers may change after
publication. Although every effort has been made to include the most up-to-date
information in this book, there can be no guarantee that this information won't
change with time.

Library of Congress Cataloging in Publication Data
  Ford, Clyde W.
    We *can* all get along : 50 steps you can take to help end racism /
  Clyde W. Ford.
      p.   cm.
    Includes bibliographical references.
    ISBN 0-440-50570-4
      1. Racism—United States.   2. United States—Race relations.
  I. Title.
  E184.A1F595   1994
  305.8'00973—dc20   93-1930
                                                              CIP

Printed in the United States of America

Published simultaneously in Canada

February 1994

10 9 8 7 6 5 4 3 2 1

FFG

Contents

For Your Family

For Your Community

Contents

Foreword

Martin Luther King III

Despite the progress that has been made in the United States toward achieving racial justice since the civil rights movement, racism remains the single most destructive force in American life. Social problems such as poverty, unemployment, urban decay, deteriorating educational opportunities, crime, and violence are all aggravated by the persistence of racism in our society.

It is important that we keep moving forward with the necessary legal reforms to reduce racial and all forms of discrimination. But there is much truth in the saying that we can't legislate an end to racism, because that can begin only in the human heart. The struggle against racism must be carried forward not only in the courts and legislative bodies, but also in our personal relationships, in our daily lives. Racism must be challenged at the dinner table, in our places of work and worship, in schools, playgrounds, the media and in every institution of our society.

My father, Martin Luther King, Jr., said that "like life, racial understanding is not something we find, but something that we must create . . . the ability to work together, to understand each other will not be found ready made, it must be created by the fact of contact."

In *We Can All Get Along: 50 Steps You Can Take to Help End Racism,* Dr. Clyde Ford provides readers with invaluable guidance for facilitating that contact and fostering greater interracial understanding, friendship, and cooperation. It includes proactive projects and activities not only to reduce racism and bigotry, but also to build the beloved community my father described in his dream for America.

Dr. Ford offers specific suggestions for challenging racism at every level, from self-analysis to international conflict. He discusses strategies for confronting destructive stereotypes and mythologies, promoting racial understanding in childrearing, the arts, and education, to name just a few areas of concern. In simple, accessible language, he stresses the vital importance of developing an interracial vision at the personal, family, community, national, and global levels.

In these pages, the careful reader will find a rich mother lode of well thought out and clearly stated advice for purging racism and prejudice from our hearts, minds, and personal relationships. I wholeheartedly recommend this long-needed book to everyone who wants to help unify America into a vibrant, multicultural sister- and brotherhood—and thereby help to heal the world.

Introduction

In the midst of the anger, violence, and confusion following the L.A. racial riots—the worst in America this century— a dazed and puzzled voice questioned whether we can all get along. We had all seen this man being beaten by police on our television sets. Now, Rodney King's question was simple and direct: "People, can we all get along."

One of the most debilitating aspects of the Los Angeles riots was a feeling of powerlessness in response to Rodney King's plea. How *can* we all get along? When faced with such an overwhelming problem as racial relations in America there is a belief that the actions of one person cannot really make a difference. *We* Can *All Get Along* was written to counter that belief. The history of the struggle to end racism in this country is illuminated by moments when one simple act moved a mountain: as when Rosa Parks in 1955 refused to move to the back of a segregated bus in Montgomery, Alabama, and thereby initiated a series of events that galvanized the black freedom movement in America.

Not only the actions, but also the attitudes, of each of us can make a difference. Racism is not just a problem "out there"—in our communities, our nation, and the world. Racism is also a problem "in here"—in ourselves and in our families. *We Can All Get Along* encourages eliminating racism by working within oneself and one's family, as well as with one's community, one's nation, and the world. The title of the book should not be misleading: eliminating racism is not a simple process. There is no easy, fifty-step solution. Throughout history a great many dedicated men and women have devoted their lives to this struggle to eliminate racism—and still that struggle continues. And yet, while eliminating racism may not be simple, many of the steps one can take toward that goal are easily described. *We Can All Get Along* presents fifty possible steps.

As you read these steps you might find something that appeals to you, piques your interest, or stimulates additional thought on a subject—and that's a place to begin. Each of the fifty steps has a short summary, statistics or other relevant facts, a list of actions you can take, and resources for further action. Each step has two main purposes: first, to help you become better informed about particular aspects of eliminating racism; and, secondly to help you design a personal action plan to work toward this goal. You will find a wide variety of information in this book, culled from the history of the black freedom movement in America, and the teachings and writings of many others who have worked, and are working, toward eliminating racism.

The major goal of *We Can All Get Along* is helping *you* to find a place to begin: that place might be within yourself and the unresolved issues of your own life, or with your children; perhaps you'll investigate fair housing practices within your community; you might even be moved to start a letter-writing campaign to your congressional representatives, or lend your efforts to a worldwide organization working to end racism.

The steps in this book are meant to appeal to a wide variety of interests—from the politically active to the parentally involved; from those interested in local issues to those focused on global concerns. It doesn't really matter where you start, it only matters that you take the first steps. For the journey to eliminate racism and uphold the dignity of all human beings is very old. Many travelers, known and unknown, have ventured this path before. We need only take up the mantle they have laid down for us. We need only follow their footsteps to continue the legacy they have left behind. We need only remember that each step we take moves this journey one step closer to its goal.

Bellingham, Washington
January 1993
Clyde W. Ford

50 Steps
You Can Take

FOR YOURSELF

Understanding Racism

Understanding racism will better equip you to take steps to eliminate it.

Racism is a complex term with many different manifestations. Understanding what racism is will help you take steps to eliminate it. In 1970 the U.S. Civil Rights Commission defined racism as:

> any attitude, action, or institutional structure which subordinates a person or group because of his or their color. Even though "race" and "color" refer to two different kinds of human characteristics, in America it is the visibility of skin color—and of other physical traits associated with particular ethnic groups—that marks individuals as "targets" for subordination by members of the white majority. This is true of Negroes, Puerto Ricans, Mexican Americans, Japanese Americans, Chinese Americans, and American Indians. Specifically, white racism subordinates members of all these other groups primarily because they are not white in color. . . .

Racism—Conscious or Unconscious?

Fortunately, blatant acts of racism are not as prevalent in America as they once were. However, the police beating of Rodney King in Los Angeles and Malik Green in Detroit; the murder of Vietnamese immigrants mistakenly thought to be "job-stealing" Japanese; and the recent rise in violent attacks on minorities by skinheads and other white supremacist groups are stark reminders of the deliberate, overt racism that still exists in this country. Racist attacks on foreigners in Germany and other European countries show that America is not alone in suffering a continuing wave of racism.

Conscious racism is easy to identify, unconscious racism is not: A black manager encounters a "glass ceiling" preventing her rise within a corporation; an Hispanic couple is puzzled when they cannot find an apartment to rent in a certain neighborhood; when asked to choose a doll most black children select a white doll as more beautiful and desirable; a family automatically assumes that property values decrease when people of color move into their neighborhood, so they immediately move to another location; a person finds it impossible to obtain a loan or insurance for a business located in a black and Hispanic neighborhood.

Unconscious racism is a by-product of beliefs that are deeply ingrained in American society and transmitted to children at a young age. Even well-intentioned people can unintentionally perpetuate racism through unconscious attitudes and actions. The difference, said one observer, is that "they generally apologize for their behavior and try to change it," while out-and-out racists do not.

Prejudice + Power = Racism

Anyone may dislike someone else because of skin color or physical characteristics. A black person may hate white people; an Hispanic may hate blacks. Such hatred on the basis of skin color is bigoted, distasteful, prejudicial, and unfair, but it is not necessarily *racist*. Racism adds power to prejudice, thereby creating the means to subordinate on the basis of color. In America the white majority has long held the political, economic, social, cultural, and psychological power to subordinate people of color.

A DEFINITION OF RACISM

Given these considerations, what's a working definition of racism? Racism is any action or attitude, conscious or unconscious, that subordinates an individual or group based on skin color or race. This subordination can be enacted individually or institutionally. The figure below is a schematic diagram of this definition of racism.

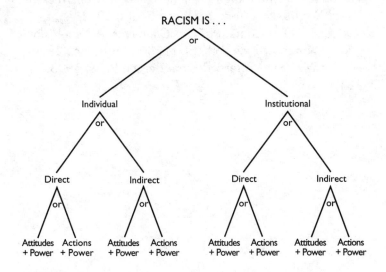

SOME RECENT BOOKS ON RACISM IN AMERICA

Bell, Derrick A. *Faces at the Bottom of the Well: The Perma-nence of Racism in America.* New York: Basic Books, Inc., 1992.

Davis, Angela Y. *Women, Culture & Politics.* New York: Random House, Inc., 1989.

Dudley, William, and Cozic, Charles, eds. *Racism in America: Opposing Viewpoints*. San Diego, CA: Greenhaven Press, Inc., 1991.

Hacker, Andrew. *Two Nations: Black and White, Separate, Hostile, Unequal*. New York: Charles Scribner's Sons, 1992.

Lang, Susan S. *Extremist Groups in America*. New York: Franklin Watts, Inc., 1990.

McKissack, Pat, and McKissack, Fredrick. *Taking a Stand Against Racism and Racial Discrimination*. New York: Franklin Watts, Inc., 1990.

Morrison, Toni, ed. *Race-ing Justice, En-Gendering Power: Essays on Anita Hill, Clarence Thomas, and the Construction of Social Reality*. New York: Pantheon Books, 1992.

Steele, Shelby. *The Content of Our Character: A New Vision of Race in America*. New York: St. Martin's Press, Inc., 1990.

West, Cornel. *Race Matters*. Boston: Beacon Press, 1993.

2

The Problem of Racism

Racism is an equal opportunity hazard.

While the effects of racism are nondiscriminatory —they involve us all—people of color have been and remain the primary "targets" of racism. Racism shapes the lives of people of color through fear of physical harm, reduction of economic and social opportunities, and the psychological burden of being viewed as inferior. But we all suffer. As a nation racism diminishes the number of people contributing to our economic and social well-being. In our personal lives racism keeps us locked into a cycle of hatred, prejudice, and anger. And in simple human terms racism ignores, devalues, and degrades the wonderful diversity of our human family.

EXAMPLES OF RACISM

- A co-worker expresses a belief that white people are genetically superior to people of color.
- Blacks are segregated in a community through the discrimina-

tory practices of real estate agents, rental agents, and mortgage lenders.

- A white acquaintance says to a person of color, "When I look
at you I don't see the color of your skin. You're just another
person like I am." However well intentioned, the underlying
message is that acceptance is based on denying rather than
embracing ethnic diversity.

- A person of color watching a television advertisement for a
new skin-care product hears, "This product is made for all
types of skin," but the commercial only shows whites.

- A white real-estate agent married to a black man is closing a
business transaction. Overnight one party to the transaction
has learned of her marriage and walks out of the closing saying, "I refuse to do business with you any longer knowing
you're married to one of them."

- A white man in Boston accuses a black man of killing his wife.
The city is outraged and the police quickly arrest a black man
who "looks like the perpetrator," according to the husband. In
reality, the white man has murdered his wife and used the
prevailing belief that blacks are likely to commit such crimes as
a cover-up.

- A white man in Cleveland is accused of abducting, sexually
assaulting, and murdering young men of color, but the police
fail to investigate the individual for over a year. When he is
arrested and they search his home, they find evidence of murder and heinous crimes primarily committed against young
men of color.

- A person of color with a four-year college degree walks into an
employment agency and is told there are no jobs available.
Moments later a white youth with a four-year college degree
walks into the same employment agency and has several interviews arranged.

- A cross is burned on the lawn of a black family recently relocated to a predominantly white neighborhood.

- While on the dance floor of a popular night club, a white man

turns to a person of color and innocently says, "You people just have a great sense of rhythm."
- Insurance companies redline a predominantly black and His-panic area of a large city so that commercial insurance rates are exorbitantly high. No businesses can afford the insurance. A fire occurs and many businesses are destroyed, leaving their owners with no means of livelihood and no way of rebuilding.
- 65% of the players in a professional sport are persons of color, 1% of the management is. "We can't find qualified people of color," say the owners.

The Goal of Ending Racism . . .

is to recognize, accept, include, honor, and celebrate the diversity of human beings. A "color-blind" or "melting-pot" society ignores the uniqueness and individuality of different people and groups. Instead we can affirm "unity in diversity." The goal of ending rac-ism is the certain knowledge that as people we are more similar than different. Our differences detract from no one, instead they benefit us all.

One Person Can Make a Difference.

We can examine ourselves, our family, our community, our nation, and the world we live in. Where we find attitudes and actions that perpetuate racism we can take steps to make a change. Regardless of color, we all have a role to play in ending racism. Our life can be an example of honoring "unity in diversity." We needn't worry about where to start. Any step toward ending racism, regardless of how small, contributes to the larger journey we must take as fami-lies, communities, and nations.

STEPS YOU CAN TAKE

- Be aware that racism is complex and affects people in many ways.

- Learn more about what racism is and how it affects people.
- Commit yourself to taking steps to eliminate racist language or assumptions in yourself, your family, your community, the nation, and the world.

REFERENCES

Bender, David L., and Bruno Leone, eds. *Racism in America: Opposing Viewpoints.* San Diego, CA: Greenhaven Press, Inc., 1991.

Katz, Judith. *White Awareness Handbook for Anti-Racism Training.* Norman, OK: University of Oklahoma Press, 1978.

Rothenberg, Paula S. *Racism and Sexism: An Integrated Study.* New York: St. Martin's Press, Inc., 1987.

U.S. Civil Rights Commission. *Racism in America and How to Combat It.* Washington, D.C.: GPO, 1970.

3

Get to Know the Changing Face of Racism

Racist behavior has declined, but racist attitudes have not.

O vert racist behavior is less socially acceptable. But there's a new racism today, based on a belief that ethnic minorities have already been given their chance to "make it" in America. If there's a problem, so this reasoning goes, it is not with white American society but with those minorities that haven't seized the opportunity.

Nowhere is this attitude more evident than toward black Americans. A majority of white Americans feel that the generation between the civil rights movement of the 1960s and the 1990s—when many discriminatory practices were legally reversed—should have been enough time for blacks to turn around a previous 350-year history of slavery, oppression, and discrimination. Blacks are compared with other ethnic minorities like Asian Americans who have come to this country and done well. "We gave them a chance," the reasoning goes. "They didn't take it; that confirms our low opinion of them, and it's no longer our responsibility to help." This new face of racism is a way of blaming the victims,

instead of identifying the continuing causes for racism and discrimination.

Such views fail to take much into account. The removal of legal
discrimination does not guarantee equal access and opportunity to
resources like education, finances, housing, and jobs. The political
will to enforce antidiscrimination and equal-opportunity legislation
has diminished in recent years. Recent decisions by a conservative
Supreme Court—once the champion of minority rights—have
eroded civil-rights gains made since the 1960s. Institutional racism
is more pervasive and more difficult to combat than overt individual
acts of racism.

Added to this new racist attitude are the shifting tactics of white
supremacist groups. No longer bent on identification with violence
and overt bigotry, white supremacist groups have donned a cloak of
respectability. Members of the KKK, for example, have dropped
their hoods for three-piece suits. These groups have also attempted
to turn the tables by portraying white Americans as an embattled
ethnic group whose very existence is challenged by other ethnic
minorities.

DID YOU KNOW[1]

- 66% of whites believe that a black person has the same chance
  of success in America as a white person.
- 77% of whites would never become romantically involved with
  a black person.
- 75% of whites say the recent success of Asian Americans confirms their low opinion of blacks.
- 68% of whites feel that some ethnic groups are simply harder
  working than others.
- 50% of whites would object to their child dating a black person.
- 50% of whites have friends who they know are racist.
- 44% of whites feel blacks are more violent than whites.
- 41% of whites are angered by the sight of a black man walking
  hand-in-hand with a white woman.

- 33% of whites feel blacks are more prone to be criminals.
- 22% of whites believe that whites are intellectually superior to blacks.
- 20% of whites feel the Ku Klux Klan has legitimate grievances.
- 19% of whites would refuse a blood transfusion from a black person.

STEPS YOU CAN TAKE

- End any denial you have about the existence of racism. Racism is alive and prevalent in America, and throughout the world, today.
- Share your awareness with others about the new face of racism.
- Learn as much as you can about the shifting tactics of actively racist groups.
- Support the efforts of organizations monitoring the activities of racist groups.

RESOURCES

- *Klan Watch,* an organization dedicated to monitoring the activities of the Ku Klux Klan and mounting legal efforts to challenge and thwart the Klan's activities.
- *Southern Poverty Law Center,* an organization that has successfully brought lawsuits against the Klan and other white supremacist groups.
- *Amnesty International,* an international organization that issues reports on the abuse of human rights throughout the world, including the United States.
- The *human rights commission* located in your state.

NOTE: *See the list of organizations at the end of steps 44 and 47 for the names and addresses of these and similar organizations.*

REFERENCES

[1]Patterson, James and Peter Kim. *The Day America Told the Truth*. New York: Prentice Hall Press, 1991.

Ridgeway, James. *Blood in the Face: The Ku Klux Klan, Aryan Nations, Nazi Skinheads, and the Rise of a New White Culture*. New York: Thunder's Mouth Press, 1991.

Rose, Douglas D. *The Emergence of David Duke and the Politics of Race*. Chapel Hill, NC: University of North Carolina Press, 1992.

4

Avoid Using
the Word *Race*

Race, as we commonly use the term, is more a
mythological creation than a scientific fact.

By definition the word *race* is divisive. The term attempts to classify subspecies of human beings according to physical characteristics such as skin color, hair texture, and size of body parts. Psychological and behavioral traits are frequently associated with these physical characteristics; and, as superior or inferior status is attributed to these traits, the term *race* becomes racist.

Scientific attempts to identify truly separate subspecies (i.e., races) of human beings have repeatedly failed, leading many scientists to conclude as early as 1936 there really was no such thing as race. Genetic differences explaining human variations in skin color, hair texture, or susceptibility to disease have been found among groups of people in different parts of the world. But genetic variations imply nothing about the superiority or inferiority of human beings. The more researchers investigate the origins of humankind the more they find we are all brothers and sisters under the skin: more similar than different; more related than separate.

DID YOU KNOW

- Historically, theoretical attempts to define racial characteristics have been thwarted by actual facts. For example, Africans were once considered the darkest-skinned people until natives in the Pacific Islands were found to have skin as dark as some Africans. Europeans had the straightest hair and thinnest noses until some of these same Pacific Islanders were found to have straight hair and thin noses.
- Blood protein matching shows Northern Europeans are physiologically closer to Africans than to Asians or Pacific Islanders.
- DNA matching shows Northern Europeans evolutionarily closer to Australian Aborigines than to Africans.
- Fossil evidence points to all human beings emerging from common ancestral stock in Africa.
- DNA fingerprinting identifies a common maternal parent for all humans on earth. Whimsically called Eve, this universal grandmother lived in Africa 150,000 to 200,000 years ago.
- The division of humankind into population groups of similar skin color, hair texture, and body characteristics (what we commonly call different races) may be a recent evolutionary phenomenon that took place perhaps only 90,000 years ago.

WHAT RESEARCHERS HAVE SAID

- "We talk all the time glibly of races and nobody can give us a definite answer to the question of what constitutes a race." *(Franz Boas, 1936)*
- "The existence of human subspecies is purely hypothetical. Nowhere does a human group now exist which corresponds closely to a systematic subspecies in animals." *(Julian Huxley and A. C. Haddon, 1936)*
- "It is customary to discuss the local variations of humanity in terms of 'race.' However, it is unnecessary to use this greatly debased word, since it is easy to describe populations without it." *(Hans Kalmus, 1958)*

- "The use of 'race' as a taxonomic [classification] unit for man seems out of date." *(J. P. Garlick, 1961)*
- "Terms should be designed to fit the facts, and not the facts forced into the procrustean rack of predetermined categories. . . . The term *race* goes far beyond the facts and only serves to obscure them." *(Ashley Montagu, 1964)*
- "There may have been a time when, on first sight, one might not have been able to distinguish a human living in what is now England from one living in what is now New Guinea." *(Michael Brown, 1990)*

STEPS YOU CAN TAKE

- Read about the origin of human beings. What emerges, despite a lingering academic controversy, is a deep sense of human oneness beyond the superficial variations we call race.
- Visit a modern museum's display on the origins of human beings. Take your children.
- Trace the possible path by which humans emerged from Africa to settle throughout the world. Look at a flat map of the world. Point to Kenya or Tanzania in East Africa. If you had to walk from there to every other major location in the world what route would you take? What climates and environments would you encounter?
- Replace the word *race* in your vocabulary with another term like *ethnic group, ethnicity, cultural background, nationality,* or *human variation* when speaking about differences among human beings. The term *race* is loaded with a history of fiction, conflict, violence, and racism. Defuse this racism by discarding this outmoded term.

REFERENCES

Brown, Michael. *The Search for Eve.* New York: Harper & Row, 1990. This is a good book for the layperson about the great debate between molecular biologists and anthropologists over our origins.

Montagu, Ashley. *The Concept of Race.* New York: Macmillan, 1964. Contains statements by prominent anthropologists debunking the commonplace notion of race. Many of the quotes cited above are from this book.

5

Use
Nonracist Language

Words help shape our ideas and beliefs about others.

Common words used to refer to people of other ethnic groups often reinforce stereotypical racist attitudes. *Black* and *white,* for example, are words with deep, abiding connotations. The *Random House Dictionary of the English Language* has a number of definitions of *black,* all negative and foreboding. For example, "soiled or stained with dirt," "gloomy, pessimistic, or dismal: *a black outlook,*" "boding ill, sullen, or hostile: *black words,*" "without any moral light or goodness; evil or wicked: *a black heart,*" "indicating censure, disgrace, etc.: *a black mark on one's record.*" Synonyms for *black: dirty, dingy, sad, depressing, somber, disastrous, calamitous,* and *sinful.*

White, on the other hand, is defined with exactly the reverse meaning. "*Slang.* honest, decent: *That's very white of you,*" "morally pure, innocent," "auspicious or fortunate," "without malice; harmless." White is worn to a wedding, for instance, black to a funeral. Substitute any definition of *black* in the phrase *black person,* then substitute any meaning of white in the phrase *white per-*

son and you will see the power of words to shape beliefs and ideas about racism.

LANGUAGE YOU CAN CHANGE

- Substitute *person(s)* or *people(s) of color* for *nonwhite*. *Nonwhite* is ethnocentric, placing "white" as a standard against which other people are judged.
- Substitute *culturally dispossessed* for *culturally deprived*. All people of color come from societies with very rich cultural traditions, though they are not European in origin. Many ethnic groups in America were forced to give up their cultural heritage and traditions.
- Substitute *economically exploited* for *economically disadvantaged*. Many people of color have a painful history of being exploited for the benefit of European Americans. Blacks were enslaved as a cheap source of labor, Chinese were imported as cheap labor, Native American land was confiscated. *Economically disadvantaged* sidesteps important issues, while *economically exploited* more accurately represents the historical plight of people of color.
- Next time you read the word *slave* substitute *Africans forcefully removed from their families and homes* or *African people held in captivity*.
- Substitute *arrival* for *discovery* when referring to Europeans like Columbus. Native Americans lived in the western hemisphere centuries before Columbus and other Europeans arrived.
- Avoid qualifiers when referring to people of different ethnic groups. For example, "We're looking for a qualified black to fill this position." The natural assumption is that everyone considered for this position should be qualified.
- Drop *pagan* when referring to the spiritual practices of traditional cultures. *Pagan* implies people who are irreligious or hedonistic. Most traditional cultures are deeply spiritual, though not in the same way as Judeo-Christian culture.

- Do not use racial epithets when referring to people of different ethnic groups.
- If you do not already know how a person of color wishes to be referred to, ask him or her.

RESOURCES

Burgest, D. "Racist Use of the English Language." *Black Scholar,* Vol. 4 (September 1973), pp. 37–45. This is a succinct article on the manner in which English perpetuates racism overtly and covertly. Many examples are given from English.

Jones, Peter. "The Language of Racism." *Scholastic Update,* April 7, 1989.

Moore, Robert B. "Racist Stereotyping in the English Language," *Racism and Sexism: An Integrated Study,* ed. P. S. Rothenberg. New York: St. Martin's Press, 1988.

Relin, David Oliver. "The Official Language of Racism." *Scholastic Update,* February 12, 1988.

Ryan, William. "Blaming the Victim." *Racism and Sexism: An Integrated Study,* ed. P. S. Rothenberg: New York: St. Martin's Press, 1988.

Rich, Evelyn Jones. "Mind Your Language," *Africa Report,* September/October 1974.

Safire, William. "Dark Words of Disapproval." *The New York Times Magazine,* January 28, 1990.

Yabura, Lloyd. "Toward a Language of Humanism," *Rhythm,* Summer 1971.

UNESCO, "Recommendations Concerning Terminology in Education on Race Questions." New York: United Nations, June 1968.

6

Inventory Your Life Experience with Racism

Discover what key personal events have shaped your experience of racism.

This Inventory of Racial Experience[1] was developed by Frederick C. Jefferson of the University of Rochester. There are two sets of parallel incidents—one for whites, the other for blacks or persons of color. The purpose of the inventory is to help you focus on those life events that have shaped your views of racism, discrimination, and related issues.

Read each item. Allow yourself time to relax and recall a specific event or situation in your life when that incident happened to you. Write down your answers with as much detail as you wish, taking into account:

- Where the incident occurred.
- Your age at the time of the incident.
- The events leading up to the incident.
- The incident itself.
- Your experience of the incident. How you felt, thought, and what you did.

- What meaning that incident has had in your life.
- What you intend to do with the meaning of that incident.

INVENTORY OF RACIAL EXPERIENCE (FOR AFRICAN AMERICANS AND OTHER PERSONS OF COLOR)

1 Discovering that being black made a difference to others.
2 Learning that blacks were slaves.
3 Becoming aware of the social position of blacks in America.
4 Wishing and hoping to be seen as equal to whites.
5 Desiring to experience acceptance and/or love from a white person.
6 Experiencing the desire to prove your equality or even superiority to whites.
7 Discovering deep resentment and distrust of other blacks.
8 Wishing that black female and/or black male intimates possessed the positive qualities of their white counterparts.
9 Discovering that a black community united in purpose can begin to crush obstacles (real and imagined) to black social, political, economic, and personal growth.
10 Deciding to actively resist those social and/or political and/or economic forces that cause feelings of powerlessness and/or worthlessness in black people.
11 Becoming aware of the desire to discover your self-power, your personhood, and ways to answer the question "Who am I?"
12 Becoming aware of the need for a spiritual center.

INVENTORY OF RACIAL EXPERIENCE (FOR WHITES)

1 Treating blacks different from whites.
2 Learning that whites created and maintained slavery in the United States.
3 Becoming aware of discrimination against blacks.

4 Feeling more fortunate than, superior to, or better than blacks.

5 Trying consciously to be especially good, kind, helpful, or loving to blacks.

6 Desiring to prove that you really are equal to or the same as blacks.

7 Being angry at other whites for what they were doing to blacks.

8 Admiring and wishing that you or whites were more like blacks in some specific way(s).

9 Feeling helpless as an individual to do anything truly useful in changing white racism.

10 Deciding to actively resist those social and/or political and/or economic forces that cause feelings of worthlessness in and subjugate black people.

11 Wanting to get over feelings of guilt and shame about being subconsciously racist.

12 Becoming aware of the need for a spiritual center.

STEPS YOU CAN TAKE

- Talk about your responses with friends and family. What thoughts, feelings, emotions surface as you review these incidents that occurred in your life? What do you value about your responses? What would you like to change?

- Modify these two inventories to encompass the experience of other peoples of color in America. Change the word *black* in the inventories to *Asians, Native Americans,* or *Hispanics.* Change item 2 in both inventories to reflect a similarly dismal experience in the history of these other peoples of color in America: Chinese mistreated as cheap, expendable laborers on the railway; Japanese Americans interned during World War II; Native Americans being forced from their land.

- If you are a person of color and have a friend who is white (or vice versa) compare the answers you both have to these twelve incidents.

REFERENCES

[1]The Inventory of Racial Experience appears in Judith H. Katz's *White Awareness: Handbook for Anti-Racism Training* (Norman, OK: University of Oklahoma Press, 1978), and is used with the permission of Frederick C. Jefferson.

7

Examine Your Personal Views About Racism

We cannot choose the color of our skin, but we can choose the nature of our beliefs.

The most difficult task of ending racism may be examining and changing personal beliefs. Few white Americans, for example, would openly admit to being racist. The term conjures up images of hate-mongering, cross-burning demagogues—images most white Americans would not identify with. Yet ask black, Hispanic, Native, or Asian Americans and you'll hear a totally different story. They will tell you the most well-meaning white Americans often commit the simplest, yet personally devastating, acts of racism.

- "I hate it when I'm told, 'I don't see you as a black person, just another individual like me,'" said a young woman of color. "Don't they [white Americans] understand what that does?" she continued. "I literally feel unseen, invalidated, and inconsequential. It's one of the most racist remarks someone can make."
- "You people—I detest that phrase," said an Asian American

man. "As though everyone with yellow skin comes from the same place, thinks the same way, has the same culture."

- "There's a real difference living in the South and living out here," remarked a Hispanic man recently relocated to a small town in the Pacific Northwest. "Back there [in Texas] people were either friendly or not. At least you knew where they stood. Out here," he continued, "I feel like an exotic visitor from another planet. People stare so hard at me I'm afraid they're going to trip because they're not looking where they're going."

- "I wish someone would see I'm Native American," said a student, "then just say to themselves, 'He's a Native American, that's great.' You know, like admiring the color of a shirt or blouse someone is wearing. . . . Then I wish they'd say to themselves, 'Now let's get on with working together, studying together, living together.' I don't like it when I'm singled out for praise or blame because of my heritage."

THE PERSONAL ROOTS OF RACISM

The roots of racism lie deeper than the inability to accept others. Racism actually begins with people who are unable to accept themselves. The historical treatment of Africans by Europeans illustrates this: puritanical sixteenth-century Europeans had great difficulty accepting their bodies. Flesh, after all, was the repository of sin, the antithesis of the Judeo-Christian ethic. So troubling aspects of the European body—sexuality, sensuality, and sanitation—were projected onto Africa, the "newly discovered 'dark continent.'"

Africans were believed to have legendary sexual prowess (a projection of European discomfort with sexuality). Africans were seen as moving their bodies in shocking ways (a projection of European discomfort with sensuality). Africans' dark skin symbolized evil, sin, and dirt (a projection of European religious beliefs). European white skin symbolized goodness, sanctity, and purity (a projection of religious beliefs). From such projections, what other conclusion should be drawn than that Africans should be conquered and dominated by

Europeans? Slavery, the slave trade, and the oppression of blacks in America were natural outgrowths of such beliefs. It is easier to project a problem onto another than to own up to it oneself.

If we don't feel good about ourselves, we won't feel good about others, particularly others who look different from us. It is often easier to project our personal problems onto other people and thereby blame them for our woes. An automobile worker experiencing personal problems because he is out of work may blame the Japanese for his personal problems. Suddenly, all Asians become targets of his hostility, and he commits acts of racist violence. Such a situation led to the death of a Vietnamese immigrant mistakenly identified as Japanese by a group of unemployed automobile workers.

Similarly, people who do not feel good about themselves look for other people they can feel superior to, and racism is born of this need for superiority. This has been a common theme among economically exploited whites in America, who harbor racist views toward blacks based on a need to believe, "We [whites] may not be doing well, but at least we're better than them [blacks]."

To end racism we not only have to change how we feel about others, we have to change how we feel about ourselves. On the one hand this means reclaiming our body, our ethnicity, and our personal history. For those who are targets of racism this also means releasing racist projections.

YOU CAN PONDER

- How comfortable are you with your body—its size and shape? How comfortable do you feel others are with your body?
- Are there aspects of how you look that you would like to change? Height, weight, size of various body parts, appearance of body parts?
- How much do you know about your ethnicity? How do you feel about your ethnic background?
- Have you ever wished you belonged to another ethnic group?
- What personal experiences do you have of being discriminated

against or victimized? What feelings still exist for you around
those experiences?

- As a person of color what's the one personal aspect of racism
  you would most like to be free of? How would your life be
  different without this aspect?
- As a European American what's the one personal aspect of
  racism you would most like to be free of? How would your life
  be different without this aspect?

8

Reclaim Your Personal History

What we try to hide about ourselves often gets misplaced onto others.

Ideally we should grow up in a loving, nurturing, supportive family, an environment that honors both our individual uniqueness and our need for a relationship with others. Unfortunately this is rarely the case. Many of us grow up in dysfunctional families crippled by addictive behavior, emotional repression, physical or sexual abuse. If the pain of our early years is not resolved we enter into adulthood with much "unfinished business."

It can be easier to blame others for our troubles, especially when those "others" look and act differently from us. The fear, anger, hatred, and mistrust that accompany racism are often expressions of unresolved personal issues. By reclaiming our personal history, however painful it may be, we can reclaim those feelings we might misplace onto others. This will not only help end racism, but bring about personal healing as well.

QUESTIONS YOU CAN ANSWER

- What major life issues are you dealing with right now?
- What are the most significant aspects of your relationship, past and present, with each of your parents, siblings, and any other important people from your childhood?
- What have been the major turning points in your life, painful and joyful?
- What are you like: what are your strengths and limitations? If you could change anything about yourself, what would that be? Why?
- How easily do you express yourself emotionally?
- What therapeutic or personal/spiritual growth processes have you gone through? How were they helpful (or not helpful) in addressing your life issues?
- What is your life purpose?

STEPS YOU CAN TAKE

- Learn as much as you can about functional and dysfunctional human relationships (read, rent a video, attend a workshop).
- Get professional therapeutic help to work with unresolved personal issues.
- Join a support group of other people working with similar issues (addiction, emotional dysfunction, sexual abuse).

ORGANIZATIONS YOU CAN CONTACT

Cocaine and Drug Abuse Hotline, (800) 662-HELP.

Institute on Black Chemical Abuse (IBCA), 2616 Nicollet Avenue South, Minneapolis, MN 55408. (612) 871-7878.

National Asian Pacific Families Against Substance Abuse (NAPAFASA), 420 E 3rd Street, Suite 909, Los Angeles, CA 90013. (213) 617-8277.

National Association of Anorexia Nervosa and Associated Disor-

ders (ANAD), Box 7, Highland Park, IL 60035. (708) 831-3438.

National Association of Lesbian and Gay Alcoholism Professionals (NALGAP), (213) 381-8524.

National Black Alcoholism Council (NBAC), 417 S. Dearborn Street, Suite 1000, Chicago, IL 60605.

National Coalition Against Domestic Violence, P.O. Box 18749, Denver, CO 80218-0749. (303) 839-1852.

Native American Association for Adult Children of Alcoholics (NAACOA), 1402 3rd Avenue, Suite 1110, Seattle, WA 98101. (206) 467-7686.

Racism and Bigotry Anonymous (RABA), a twelve-step program for persons dealing with the damaging personal effects of racism. 256 Farallones, San Francisco, CA 94112-2939. (415) 587-4207.

9

Release
the Stereotypes
You Have of Others

Our stereotypical views of others perpetuate
racism, blame the victims, and often reflect
unresolved views we have of ourselves.

Ideally, ethnic stereotypes are a way of reducing the
tension caused by the presence of members of different ethnic
groups. While the goal is admirable—reduction of tension—the
method of obtaining that goal simply perpetuates racism. Stereotypes often function to blame the victims of racism and thereby
reduce feelings of guilt and responsibility on the part of perpetra-
tors. During slavery, for example, African Americans held in captivity were often portrayed as happy, contented children who bene-
fited from the care of their captors.

Recently in a large urban area several newly unemployed automobile workers encountered a Vietnamese immigrant. Believing
him to be Japanese, and blaming all Japanese for the loss of their
jobs, they proceeded to assault this man.

Another example: A white American male insecure about his
economic future blames his feelings of powerlessness on welfare
recipients too lazy to work and looking for a free ride. The stereotypical view of a welfare recipient is a single black mother, so this

man assumes that poor black women are his enemies. (The irony is that many more whites than people of color are welfare recipients.)

One way of ending our stereotypes of others is by acknowledging, accepting, and actively working to change the unresolved feelings of anger, guilt, responsibility, and powerlessness that we have. Thus, we can own our part in bringing an end to racism.

DID YOU KNOW[1]

- 61% of whites thinks blacks are naturally athletic.
- 33% of whites believe blacks are more likely to be criminals.
- 32% of whites feel blacks are more likely to be poor.
- 30% of whites see blacks as dangerous.
- 29% of whites feel blacks are lazy.
- 22% of whites view blacks as vulgar.
- 14% of whites think blacks are dirty.

- 49% of blacks feel all whites are racist.
- 29% of blacks believe whites are wealthy.
- 21% of blacks think whites are greedy.
- 14% of blacks view whites as intelligent.
- 14% of blacks feel whites are dangerous.

STEPS YOU CAN TAKE

1 Acknowledge your stereotypical views. From the List of Descriptive Words at the end of this section, select five that describe your stereotypical views of another ethnic group.
2 Verbalize your stereotypes. Say out loud, or silently to yourself, "I believe (_name of ethnic group_) to be (_stereotypical word_)." Repeat this for each word you selected.
3 What's it like to hear yourself verbalize these views?
4 Own your projection. Now transpose each sentence by saying, "This belief about (_stereotypical view_) comes from an attitude I have about myself." Do this for each word you selected, pausing to find the truth in each new statement you make. For example,

one person at a workshop on racism expressed the stereotypical belief that blacks were lazy. When asked to reflect on the personal roots of that belief he observed that he was a workaholic who judged others based on how much he worked.

5 What's it like to realize your stereotypes stem from beliefs you have about yourself? How might you change those personal beliefs? How might changing your personal beliefs affect the beliefs you have about others?

REFERENCES

[1]Patterson and Kim, op. cit.
Katz, op. cit.

LIST OF DESCRIPTIVE WORDS

abused	cool	humble
afraid	courageous	hurt
angry	cultured	independent
apathetic	defensive	inferior
arrogant	demanding	innocent
ashamed	derogatory	insensitive
attractive	deserving	insulted
bad	dignified	insulting
beautiful	dirty	intellectual
bigoted	educated	intelligent
blamed	emotional	invisible
brave	enraged	liberal
caring	fair	logical
Christian	fearful	mean
clean	friendly	misinformed
compassionate	good	naive
confident	guilty	non-Christian
conservative	happy	offensive
controlled	helpless	oppressed

oppressive	pushy	tokenized
outraged	respected	ugly
pagan	responsible	unattractive
patient	rich	underprivileged
peaceful	scary	undeserving
poor	secure	unemotional
powerful	sensual	unfair
powerless	sexual	untrustworthy
prejudiced	sinful	victimized
primitive	smart	violent
privileged	soulful	vulgar
proud	stupid	worthless
pure	superior	worthy

NOTE: *Add to this list any word that does not appear but represents a belief you have about yourself or someone of another ethnic group.*

10

Release
the Stereotypes
You Have of Yourself

Stereotypes can become part of one's self-image.

P_{art} of the insidious nature of racism is that stereotypes can be incorporated into one's self-image. If a person hears often enough that he is lazy, that message may become part of his internal reality. Two responses are possible: that person may attempt to live up to the internalized message of laziness, or he may continually rebel against that message. In either case that individual's behavior is influenced by the stereotype. To break the cycle of racism and despair we need to be able to acknowledge and release the racist stereotypes we have taken on and retained.

STEPS YOU CAN TAKE

1 Acknowledge the stereotypical views you have of yourself. From the List of Descriptive Words at the end of the previous section, select five that describe stereotypical views you have of yourself *based on your ethnicity.*

2 Verbalize your stereotypes. Say out loud, or silently to yourself, "I

believe myself to be (*stereotypical word*)." Repeat this for each word you selected.

3 What's it like to hear yourself verbalize these views?

4 Release the projections of others. Now transpose each sentence by saying, "This belief about (*stereotypical view*) comes from an attitude others may have about me. I now release this view of myself." Do this for each word you selected, pausing to find the truth in each new statement you make.

5 What's it like to realize the beliefs you have about yourself may stem from the beliefs others have about you? Other than verbalizing your willingness to let go of these stereotypes of yourself, what are some other ways you can release these unwanted personal beliefs?

11

Use Humor That Helps, Not Humor That Hurts

Humor at the expense of others is hurtful, often doing nothing more than reinforcing racist stereotypes.

Told worldwide, ethnic jokes usually demean members of a minority group, who are portrayed in some outlandish way as stupid, cowardly, sexually promiscuous, incompetent, or unfit to be part of the larger social order. Ethnic jokes most often support the status quo by reinforcing racist stereotypes of minorities. They are a modified form of aggression—instead of being physically struck, the victim is butted with the joke—and in this way the joke is racist. The joke teller is relieved from directly confronting the falsehood of ethnic stereotypes, and instead is reassured that the stereotype is correct. Ethnic jokes directed at blacks, for example, were used extensively by whites in the South during slavery and afterwards as a means of psychologically supporting the inferior status and treatment of blacks in America.

Humor also has a positive role in ending racism. Ethnic groups frequently use intragroup jokes to reinforce a sense of community, identity, and uniqueness. Humor can be directed at those who resist change and cling to racist stereotypes. Humor can highlight the absurdity of differences between human beings, and the strange ways we deal with those differences. Humor can lighten the heaviness of racism. Finally, humor can be used to promote a vision of a nonracist society.

STEPS YOU CAN TAKE

- Determine not to tell ethnic jokes in which a minority is demeaned. Many local, state, and federal laws covering workplace discrimination consider the telling of ethnic jokes to be proof of discrimination because it creates a hostile climate for the member of an ethnic group to work in. See step 31 for additional information.
- Let people know you're not interested in hearing demeaning ethnic jokes. If they persist in a workplace, report the offenders to a supervisor. Being forced to listen to an offensive ethnic joke is a violation of your civil rights. See step 31 for additional information.
- Create jokes that counter racism. The Australian Human Rights Commission's "Different Colors, One People" campaign recently announced a special award for Australia's best antiracist joke.
- Find the nonracist humor in ethnic differences: for example, it's ironic that many people with light skin and straight hair discriminate against people with dark skin and curly hair, then turn around to spend great sums of money darkening their skin in a tanning parlor and curling their hair at the hairdresser.
- Listen to the humor of other ethnic groups with care and sensitivity. Whether you read a book of ethnic humor or listen to a stand-up comedian, humor can help you learn about the impact of racism on an ethnic minority, and how that group has coped with bigotry and discrimination. But humor can also be deeply irresponsible by reinforcing negative racist stereotypes. Be discriminating with ethnic humor—embrace humor that encourages diversity and helps eliminate racist stereotypes, reject humor that promotes racism.
- Use the proverbs and witticisms of other ethnic groups. Learn-

ing and using a wisdom tradition different from our own can help penetrate the barriers of racism. Proverbs, for example, are encapsulated portions of a culture's philosophy of life. Through them you can discover how other people deal with universal life situations. You'll find the similarities surprising and the differences refreshing. You might even discover new ideas for approaching situations that arise in your life.

ETHNIC PROVERBS YOU CAN USE

- A good thing sells itself, a bad thing wants advertising. (African)
- When two elephants struggle, the grass suffers. (African)
- The house of the heart is never full. (African)
- The crown of good disposition is humility. (Arabic)
- A house established by oppression cannot enjoy the fruits of oppression long. (Chinese)
- Tell me who you are going around with, and I'll tell you who you are. (Hispanic)
- Fate assists the courageous. (Japanese)
- It is one life whether we spend it laughing or crying. (Japanese)
- Tap even a stone bridge before crossing. (Korean)

ANTIRACIST JOKES

What is the difference between a racist and a fish? One is wet and slimy and the other is a fish.

Why are most racially prejudiced jokes one-liners? So racists can understand them.

REFERENCES

Buchanan, Daniel Crump. *A Collection of Irish Proverbs.* Norman, OK: University of Oklahoma Press, 1965.

Hart, Henry Hersch. *Seven Hundred Chinese Proverbs.* Stanford, CA: Stanford University Press, 1937.

King, Anita. *Quotations in Black*. Westport, CT: Greenwood Press, 1981.

Lamont-Brown, Raymond. *A Book of Proverbs*. New York: Taplinger Publication Co., 1970.

Rivera, Tomás. *Y No Se lo Tragó la Tierra (And the Earth Did Not Swallow Him Up)*. Houston: Arte Publico, 1986.

Whiting, Bartlett Jere. *Modern Proverbs and Proverbial Sayings*. Cambridge, MA: Harvard University Press, 1989.

Zona, Guy. *The House of the Heart Is Never Full and Other Proverbs of Africa*. New York: Touchstone Books, 1993.

12

Zero Tolerance
for Racism

Develop a personal attitude of absolutely no
tolerance for racism.

The history of racism shows that leaving biased
comments and bigoted acts unchallenged sends a tacit message of
approval. Develop zero tolerance for racism that affects you personally, regardless of how small the incident may seem. At a consumer's cooperative one member was frequently observed harassing shoppers with racist remarks and threatening gestures. It went
on for several years tolerated by workers at the cooperative, board
members, and the general public. Some people were afraid to say
anything, while others were content to let these incidents pass by as
just the actions of a "sick individual."

Finally a person of color who belonged to the cooperative could
no longer tolerate these racist confrontations. He brought his concerns to the board. The cooperative had a chance to examine its
policies regarding racism, and the offending member was denied
his membership and no longer welcomed at the establishment. Tol-
erating racism reinforces racism. Speak out, challenge what offends
you, and send a message to others that you have zero tolerance for
racism.

DID YOU KNOW[1]

- 77% of people feel that family values are the primary reason prejudice is passed from one generation to the next.
- 65% of people believe personal experience is the primary factor in passing along prejudice.
- 57% of people thought the school environment was the main reason for intergenerational prejudice.
- 52% of people said that the workplace was the principal cause of passing prejudice along.

STEPS YOU CAN TAKE

- Learn to confront a racist remark. When you hear a bigoted remark say something as simple as "I find what you're saying offensive (or disgusting). Please keep your views to yourself."
- Racist remarks in the workplace are forbidden under civil rights laws. Inform your co-workers you do not wish to work in an environment where racist remarks are uttered. See step 31 for additional information.
- If racist remarks continue in the workplace, keep a record and report them to a supervisor or the equal opportunity office. If need be contact your state human rights commission to report workplace racism. See step 31 for additional information.
- Report racist incidents, regardless of how inconsequential, to appropriate local authorities like the police or human rights commission. Filing a complaint may help to strengthen a pending legal case against an individual or organization accused of racist activities.

REFERENCES

[1]From a survey conducted by *McCall's* magazine after the violence in Los Angeles following the verdict in the Rodney King case. Statistics appear in *McCall's,* August 1992, p. 74.

Fitzpatrick, Jean Grasso. "Can We All Get Along?" *McCall's* (August 1992).

13

Develop
Cross-Cultural
Communication Skills

Learn to communicate across cultural and ethnic lines.

We ordinarily assume that most people are "just like us." While this is true for many aspects of being human, culture and ethnicity demonstrate human uniqueness and difference. When we expect others to be "just like us," and they aren't, we can get caught in a cultural gap: something is said that offends us; someone acts in a way that shocks or angers us; another response causes us fear. One reaction is to pull back and withdraw into what is familiar and acceptable. This reaction, however, does not further communication; instead, it often gives rise to racist attitudes, actions, and beliefs. Discovering that others are "not just like us" can create a boundary between "them" and "us." Across this boundary, stereotypical labeling is substituted for real communication; honest human interchange is replaced by reactions based on anger, fear, and unresolved emotions.

There are other options when we come upon unexpected cultural interchanges. We can simply become aware of our reaction, whatever that reaction is: fear, anger, frustration, being offended. Without withdrawing we can observe our reaction and its source—

our preconditioned expectations and beliefs. This awareness can lead us to change how we interact with others; and we can develop more realistic expectations about communicating with people from different cultural backgrounds.

But awareness does not come without work. Since it runs against what we have been taught throughout our life, we have to cultivate the art of being aware in the process of communicating with others. In other words, awareness of our reactions to others is something we need to practice. Through this awareness we can readjust how we interact with others. We can accept others because we can accept ourselves. We can honor human differences through our awareness, and through our ability to change how we interact with people from other cultures and ethnic groups.

DID YOU KNOW[1]

In one study a group of African Americans identified seven major determinants of satisfying communication with whites:

- The degree of *negative stereotyping* involved in conversations. This included forms of "indirect stereotyping" like talking about "black topics" (such as music or sports) or assuming that any African American represented the views of all African Americans. Minimal negative stereotyping was more satisfying.
- How much *acceptance* they felt for their expressed feelings and opinions.
- The amount of *emotional expressiveness.* Greater emotional expressiveness was linked to more satisfying interethnic communication.
- *Authenticity,* or the degree to which these African Americans could "be themselves" in conversation with whites. Satisfying communication went along with higher degrees of authenticity.
- *Understanding.* When respondents felt understood, good communication was reported.
- *Goal attainment.* Satisfactory communication frequently re-

sulted in problem solving, information exchange, or the completion of a project.

- _Powerlessness._ When respondents felt controlled, trapped, or manipulated, poor communication was described. Some examples: when the conversation was "hogged" by the other person; when someone attempted to persuade them through aggressive or subtle tactics; when they were repeatedly interrupted.

STEPS TO COMMUNICATING CROSS-CULTURALLY

- _Build mutual understanding_ rather than trying to understand where another is "coming from." No one is really able to "walk in another person's shoes." When we try to understand where someone is "coming from," we end up superimposing our life experience on theirs.
- _Be open-minded._ Accept your views as just one of many possible filters on reality, while accepting someone else's views as just another filter on reality.
- _Bridge differences_ rather than insist on similarity of views.
- _Seek agreement through synthesis_ rather than taking sides. Instead of giving up your views, or asking others to give up theirs, find a third position that offers common ground between differing views. This results in a cocreated, or shared, reality.
- _Focus on the relationship_ rather than the individual parties to the relationship. Instead of being concerned with "what I said" and "what was said to me," be aware of the quality of the communication that takes place. In other words, move beyond "self" and "other" and focus on the interaction that takes place while communicating.
- Learn to hold the parties you communicate with in the _highest positive regard._ You may not agree with or fully understand the other person, but you can allow him or her to be with whatever feeling or thought is present in the moment—confu-

sion, resentment, anger, courage, or love. This is holding someone in the highest positive regard: You accept and respect whatever he or she communicates without trying to change, control, or alter that communication.

REFERENCES

Broome, Benjamin. "Building Shared Meaning: Implications of a Relational Approach to Empathy for Teaching Intercultural Communication." *Communication Education,* Vol. 40 (July 1991).

[1]Hecht, Michael L., Sidney Ribeau, and J. K. Alberts. "An Afro-American Perspective on Interethnic Communication." *Communication Monographs,* Vol. 56 (December 1989).

Rogers, Carl. *On Personal Power.* New York: Delacorte Press, 1977.

Storti, Craig. *The Art of Crossing Cultures.* New York: Intercultural Press, Inc., 1989.

14

Invest in Eliminating Racism

Put your money where your beliefs are.

The money you invest affects lives. It can be used for a development project in a country creating jobs for people, or it can fund a corrupt government in a country that flagrantly violates human rights. Your money can be reinvested in gold that comes from a country with a racist government, or used to support a cooperative farming project that feeds a whole village. It can be used by a bank to invest in businesses in a minority ethnic community, or invested only in more affluent, predominantly white communities.

Don't be fooled—socially conscious investing yields attractive rates of return. A recent study compared several socially conscious mutual funds and found their rates of return were equal to—and a few better than—the average mutual fund. For 1991 the Domini Index of Socially Conscious Stocks gained 19% while the Dow Jones Stock Index gained 18%. Put your money where your beliefs are. Consult the list of socially conscious investment institutions at the end of this chapter. Find out how your investments are being used and invest in ways that help to eliminate racism.

STEPS YOU CAN TAKE

- Ask both your local commercial bank and your local savings bank or credit union what percentage of their funds are invested in low-income, minority communities.
- Switch your mutual funds to a socially conscious mutual fund.
- Examine the annual report of corporations you invest in. Determine where they are reinvesting funds. Ask questions at the stockholder meeting. Write a letter requesting investment information to the corporation executive responsible for funds investment.
- If you feel a bank or corporation is investing in ways that contribute to racism (investing in a country with a poor human rights record, no investment in minority communities), write a letter and voice your opinion to that institution's investment officer. If the institution's explanation is unsatisfactory, or the institution is unwilling to change, move your money somewhere else and write a letter explaining why.
- Tell your broker or financial planner that you are interested in socially conscious investments.
- Get a VISA or Master Card from an organization that actively works to end racism and human rights violations. This is called an *affinity card,* where a certain percentage of the funds collected are used for the organization's goals. (See references below.)
- Give charitable, tax-deductible donations to organizations that work to eliminate racism.

REFERENCES (BOOKS)

Alperson, Myra, et al. *The Better World Investment Guide: One Hundred Companies Whose Policies You Should Know About.* Englewood Cliffs, NJ: Prentice-Hall Press, 1991.

Brill, Jack A., and Alan Reder. *Investing from the Heart: The Guide to Socially Responsible Investments and Money Management.* New York: Crown Publishers, Inc., 1992.

Bruyn, Severyn T. *The Field of Social Investment.* London: Cambridge University Press, 1987.

Domini, Amy L., and Peter D. Kimber. *Ethical Investing: How to Make Profitable Investments Without Sacrificing Your Principles.* New York: Addison-Wesley Publishing Co., Inc., 1986.

Harrington, John. *Investing with Your Conscience.* New York: John Wiley & Sons, Inc., 1992.

Judd, Elizabeth. *Investing with a Social Conscience.* New York: Pharos Books, 1990.

Lydenberg, Steven, et al. *Rating America's Corporate Conscience.* New York: Addison-Wesley Publishing Co., Inc., 1986.

Meeker-Lowry, Susan. *Economics as If the Earth Really Mattered: A Catalyst Guide to Socially Conscious Investing.* Philadelphia: New Society Publishers, 1988.

REFERENCES (PERIODICALS)

Corporate Responsibility Monitor. Interfaith Center on Corporate Responsibility, 475 Riverside Drive, Room 566, New York, NY 10115. (212) 870-2295.

Good Money, Box 363, Worcester, VT 05682. (802) 223-3911.

National Boycott Newsletter, Institute for Consumer Responsibility, 6505 28th Avenue, NE, Seattle, WA 98115.

News for Investors, Investor Responsibility Research Center, 1755 Massachusetts Avenue, NW, Washington, D.C. 20036. (202) 234-7500.

Social Issues Service. Investor Responsibility Research Center, 1755 Massachusetts Avenue, NW, Washington, D.C. 20036. (202) 234-7500.

South Africa Review Service. Investor Responsibility Research Center, 1755 Massachusetts Avenue, NW, Washington, D.C. 20036. (202) 234-7500. Examines legal and economic actions that may affect investments and investors in South Africa.

SOCIALLY CONSCIOUS INVESTMENT ORGANIZATIONS

The Calvert Group, 4550 Montgomery Avenue, Suite 1000N Bethesda, MD 20814. (800) 368-2748. Full range of socially conscious investments—stocks, bonds, mutual funds, money-market.

Coastal Enterprises, Box 268, Wiscasset, ME 04578. (207) 882-7552. Community-development corporation for financial and technical assistance to low-income families through business loans, social services, and housing.

Covenant Portfolio. A load mutual fund. (800) 833-4909.

Domini Social Index Trust. A no-load mutual fund. (800) 762-6814.

F. L. Putnam Investment Management Company. 10 Langley Road, Newton Centre, MA 02159. (800) 344-3435. Full range of socially conscious investment options.

First Affirmative Financial Network, 1040 S. 8th Street, Suite 200, Colorado Springs, CO 80906. (800) 422-7284. Full range of socially conscious investment options.

Green Century Funds, 29 Temple Place, Suite 200, Boston, MA 02111. (800) 934-7336. Environmentally conscious mutual fund.

Harrington Investments, 1001 Second St., Suite 325, Napa, CA 94559. (800) 788-0154. Investment services from a founder of Working Assets, John Harrington.

Pax World Fund, 224 State Street, Portsmouth, NH 03801. (800) 767-1729. Socially conscious mutual fund.

Working Assets, 701 Montgomery Street, San Francisco, CA 94111. (800) 847-7378. Supplies a traditional VISA card and long-distance phone service with a percentage of the assets going to groups working for peace, human rights, and environmental safeguards.

15

Use Your
Personal Computer

Go "on-line" with your efforts to eliminate racism.

The widespread existence of home computers and worldwide computer networks links us together in an "electronic global village." If your home computer is equipped with a modem you can participate in this global electronic community, giving you instant access to people and information, two valuable resources in bringing an end to racism. Your computer communicates with the network through your telephone line. From on-line networks you can learn about national and global efforts aimed at countering and eliminating racism, participate in discussions on this topic, and take specific actions to contribute to ongoing efforts in this area.

In the Industrial Age power was distributed between the "haves" and the "have-nots," but in the present Information Age, power is increasingly distributed between the "knows" and the "know-nots." Information is power: the power of being informed, the power of being connected with others, the power to make decisions, the power to take action. Harness this power in ending racism.

STEPS YOU CAN TAKE USING YOUR PERSONAL COMPUTER

- Join a computer network where people strive to eliminate racism. Network user fees are reasonable; often there is no cost for the telephone call. There may be network usage charges, which generally average under ten dollars per hour but rarely do you need to spend an entire hour. You can access the network, gather the information that interests you, have the network load it onto your home computer, then get off the network—a process taking only a couple of minutes. Then at your own pace you can read through the material and write responses on your computer. You can then get back on the network and place your responses so other members can read them. Again, this process only takes a couple of minutes. Several networks are listed at the end of this step.
- Gain access to national and global news about events related to eliminating racism. You can frequently obtain news reports that will never appear on network radio or television news programs. A major wire service like the Associated Press transmits many news stories to large media organizations that are not used because of space and time restrictions. These same news stories are also transmitted to computer networks where you may find them. Computer networks may be the only place you can find the reports of many smaller news organizations with specific interests in the rights and affairs of ethnic minorities.
- Examine reference materials (encyclopedia entries, articles, news clippings) related to ending racism.
- Join an issues forum and discuss eliminating racism with people throughout the world. Right after the Los Angeles riots members of one computer network opened an electronic forum to discuss thoughts, feelings, and ideas about racism and ways to end it.
- Develop a network of like-minded individuals working to eliminate racism. In network terminology these support groups are called "forums" or "conferences" and may involve many peo-

ple spread throughout the world who communicate with each other electronically. Several panelists at a large face-to-face conference on racism spent six months before the gathering communicating with each other through a computer network. Though they had never met each other, by the time of the conference they were thoroughly familiar with each other's ideas. Instead of getting to know each other at the conference they spent more time focusing on their common goal of finding ways to eliminate racism.

- Learn the views of national and global leaders on issues related to ending racism. During the 1992 presidential campaign some candidates created forums where network users could ask questions of the candidate and learn the candidates' views on important issues.
- Electronically send letters, telegrams, or faxes to local, state, national, and global political leaders expressing your views about eliminating racism.
- Obtain guidance and support for a personal or community project from people who have undertaken such projects themselves. Have a question about organizing a local event? Need some artwork to create a flyer for your event? Want to speak to someone about the ins and outs of getting laws through a city council? Simply broadcast your message over a computer network, and you can get responses from people throughout the world.
- Join a global organization working to eliminate racism. Often you can join an organization right through the network.
- Respond to an Urgent Action (UA) appeal. Amnesty International electronically posts UAs on events taking place around the world—for example, arrests of political prisoners, the activities of death squads, police brutality incidents. From your computer screen you can review the event and examine the position taken by Amnesty International. Then, if you would like to support that position, you can compose a fax or telegram at your computer that will be sent to the appropriate person or

agency over the network. The whole process takes just a few minutes.

RESOURCES

CompuServe, 5000 Arlington Centre Blvd., Columbus, OH 43220. (800) 544-1224. This is one of the oldest and largest computer networks with links throughout the world. There is a reasonable connect time fee and the telephone call is often to a local number. You can use the extensive set of services provided by CompuServe or use the network to locate related smaller networks or computer bulletin boards in your area. Amnesty International posts Urgent Action (UA) appeals and information related to human rights on the Issues Forum of CompuServe.

The Meta Network, 2000 N. 15th St., Suite 103, Arlington, VA 22201. (703) 247-8301. A global access network focusing on issues of personal and social change. The Meta Network conferences address issues of social justice, support organizations working for social change, and provide electronic gateways to other networks throughout the world.

PeaceNet, 18 De Boom Street, San Francisco, CA 94107. (415) 442-0220. PeaceNet and its companion network EcoNet are members of an international confederation of network users known as APC (the Association for Progressive Communication), which includes ConflictNet, Web, NordNet, GreenNet, Pegasus, ComLink, AlterNex, Nicarao, Huracan, Ecuanex, and GlasNet. There are more than sixteen thousand members of APC in ninety-four countries. PeaceNet was formed to address issues of world peace and social justice. The PeaceNet forum on racism contains entries on a wide array of subjects: current events, historical accounts, essays, position papers, calls for action. Entries come from concerned individuals and organizations throughout the world.

PeaceNet also maintains InterACT, a service for helping network users communicate with elected representatives, world leaders, and the media. Telephone and fax numbers for all members of the U.S. House of Representatives, the U.S. Senate, major media organizations, missions of the United Nations member countries, and other key international agencies and individuals are stored on a PeaceNet database. For less than the cost of a telephone call PeaceNet will electronically send your message via fax to any of these sources.

Prodigy, 445 Hamilton Ave, White Plains, NY 10601. (800) 776-0840, is a large-scale network similar to CompuServe.

Sphinx Communications Group, 1729 21st St., NW Washington, D.C. 20009. (202) 986-3654, and the affiliated *National Black Communications Network (NABCON)* have conferencing and network services that support a number of individual and national organizations working to eliminate racism.

16

Learn the History of Ethnic Minorities

Learn more about different ethnic groups by learning about their history.

All ethnic groups exhibit a pride rooted in their history. Yet for many Americans, non-European ethnic minorities are just a footnote in American history. Only recently have textbooks begun a nonracist treatment of American history. Still, much of the real history of America is found outside the mainstream belief that white American men were the main movers of this country. Much of the real history of the world is found outside the dominant belief that Europe was the main center of world civilization. Learning about the history and contributions of all ethnic groups to your community, nation, and world is a step taken toward eliminating racism.

Facing historical truth is an important part of learning the history of ethnic minorities. The history of every ethnic group holds stories of sorrows and tragedies suffered because of racism in America. These tragic moments are part of the shameful, and often untold, story of America. For ethnic minorities they are also rallying points: times never to forget, times when an ethnic group pulled together to weather injustice, times when a hero arose to lead the group forward, times when lives were lost in the struggle for freedom, justice, and equal opportunity in America. Americans must embrace all of their history—the joy and the sorrow; the glory and suffering; the triumph and the tragedy. Facing history is a step toward eliminating racism.

A FEW HISTORICAL FACTS EVERYONE SHOULD KNOW

- More than 20 million Africans were killed, or died, in the Middle Passage of the slave trade, a route from West Africa to the West Indies and the United States.
- The Chinese Exclusion Act of 1882 forbade the immigration of Chinese people to America.
- Several hundred Chinese were killed in the late 1800s during riots that erupted while they were demonstrating for more jobs.
- In order to prevent newly freed slaves from voting, many southern states levied prohibitive poll taxes, or required African Americans, and them alone, to recite verbatim the Declaration of Independence or the Constitution of the United States under the guise of voting "qualifications."
- Immigration laws of the 1920s barred Japanese immigrants as "aliens ineligible for citizenship."
- 120,000 Japanese American citizens were illegally interned by the United States government during World War II as potential traitors and threats to national security.
- With the signing of the Treaty of Guadalupe Hidalgo in 1848, which ended the Mexican War, the United States took from Mexico what is now California, Arizona, New Mexico, Nevada, Colorado, Utah, and parts of Wyoming. Anglos moving into those newly acquired territories stole land, killed Mexicans, and drove them out, even though rights of ownership were guaranteed to Mexicans by the treaty.
- America was slow to accept reports of the genocide of Jews by

Germany during World War II, and even slower to allow Jews facing torture and death to immigrate to this country.
* Immigration policies still smack of racism today as Haitian boat people are turned away, and even a major 1992 presidential candidate suggested building a fence along the Mexican-American border.

REFERENCES ON THE HISTORY OF ETHNIC MINORITIES IN AMERICA

Bennett, Lerone, Jr. *Before the* Mayflower: A History of Black America. Chicago: Johnson Publishing Co., Inc. 1988.

Chen, Jack. *The Chinese of America*. San Francisco: Harper & Row, 1980.

Daniels, Roger. *Coming to America: A History of Immigration and Ethnicity in American Life*. New York: HarperCollins Publishers, Inc., 1990.

Deloria, Vine. *We Talk, You Listen; New Tribes, New Turf*. New York: Macmillan Publishing Co., Inc., 1970.

Franklin, John Hope. *From Slavery to Freedom: A History of Negro Americans*. New York: Alfred A. Knopf, Inc., 1988.

Garver, Susan, and Paula McGuire. *Coming to North America: From Mexico, Cuba, and Puerto Rico*. New York: Delacorte Press, 1981.

Gomez, David F. *Somos Chicanos: Strangers in Our Own Land*. Boston: Beacon Publishing, 1973.

Harding, Vincent. *There Is a River: The Black Struggle for Freedom in America*. New York: Harcourt Brace Jovanovich Inc., 1981.

Josephy, Alvin M. *America in 1492: The World of the Indian Peoples before the Arrival of Columbus*. New York: Alfred A. Knopf, Inc., 1992.

Takaki, Ronald T. *A Different Mirror: A History of Multicultural America*. Boston: Little Brown, 1993.

Takaki, Ronald T. *Strangers from a Different Shore: A History of Asian Americans*. Boston: Little Brown, 1989.

Tsai, Shih-shan Henry. *The Chinese Experience in America.* Bloomington, IN: Indiana University Press, 1986.

Wagenheim, Kal, and Olga Jiménez de Wagenheim. *The Puerto Ricans: A Documentary History.* New York: Praeger Publishers, 1973.

Weatherford, J. McIver. *Native Roots: How the Indians Nourished America.* New York: Crown Publishers, Inc., 1991.

Wilson, Robert A. and Bill Hosokawa. *East to America: A History of the Japanese in the United States.* New York: William Morrow and Co., Inc., 1980.

RESOURCES

- Your local library will have a complete list of books, audiotapes, and videotapes you might borrow or rent to learn about the history of ethnic minorities. An example of an excellent videotape on African American history is the Public Broadcasting Service's videotape series entitled *Eyes on the Prize.* PBS Video, 1320 Braddock Place, Alexandria, VA 22314.

17

Develop a New Mythology of Black and White

Racism survives, in part, because of a cultural mythology about black and white.

The segregation of people into white and black fits a deep Western cultural mythology. In the West black has long symbolized Evil and white has symbolized Good. These colors are metaphors for the many dualities of Western culture: Mind vs. Body, Good vs. Evil, God vs. Man, Salvation vs. Sin, Cleanliness vs. Uncleanness, Man vs. Woman, Fullness vs. Emptiness, Love vs. Fear. These dualities form the basis of Judeo-Christian thought from which Western civilization emerged. From these dualities come Western ethics: morality, spirituality, law, forms of government, and social organization. The underlying theme is one of opposition and conquest: Good must triumph over Evil, "white" must conquer "black."

Thus when white European culture met black African culture the results were nearly predictable. For Europe this was a mythological battle par excellence, and Good *could* vanquish Evil: the drama was real, the players were flesh and bone, the results of the conquest could be captured, displayed, and even sold. This mythology of black and white is so deeply rooted in Western thought that few even question its existence. Yet it is at the heart of most conscious and unconscious racist attitudes and actions.

Joseph Campbell, the famed historian of mythology, lamented our lack of a modern mythology. "The story that we have in the West," noted Campbell, "is based on a view of the universe that belongs to the first millennium B.C. It does not accord with our concept either of the universe or of the dignity of man. It belongs entirely somewhere else." Franz Fanon, the African psychiatrist who studied the effects of French colonization and oppression on people of color, also called for a new mythology: "Come, brothers, for Europe and for ourselves let us turn over a new leaf and create a new model of man no longer shaped in the European tradition of racism and oppression." Eliminating racism calls for the adoption of such a new cultural mythology.

Old Cultural Mythology	**New Cultural Mythology**
White (Good) is in conflict with Black (Evil). _Oppositoria Oppositorium_ (the opposition of opposites).	White implies both Good and Evil, Black implies both Good and Evil. _Coincidentia Oppositorium_ (the union of opposites).
Manifest Destiny, the inevitable progress and conquest of North America by white Americans.	Manifold Destiny, the inevitable progress and inclusion of all Americans in North America.
The American "melting pot." Ethnic differences are homogenized into one mainstream American identity.	The American "mosaic." Ethnic differences are woven into a tapestry of American identities.
America as a "color-blind" society that sees no differences.	America as a "rainbow-conscious" society that embraces and values differences.
Us (white Americans) versus Them (minorities, Americans of color).	We (Americans of all colors) need each other.

Old Cultural Mythology	**New Cultural Mythology**
Third World people of color are primitive and pagan.	Third World people of color are culturally different and deeply spiritual.
Difference—skin color, language, beliefs, and customs—threatens traditional beliefs and values.	Difference—skin color, language, beliefs, and customs—makes us richer; it should be celebrated.

STEPS YOU CAN TAKE

- Learn more about how our current cultural mythology of black and white enables the continuation of racism. Author Toni Morrison discusses this in her book *Whiteness and the Literary Imagination* (Cambridge, Mass.: Harvard University Press, 1992).
- Eliminate language that continues the old cultural mythology of black and white. See step 5 for additional information.
- Draw on non-European, nonracist sources that support the new cultural mythology of black and white.
- Develop cross-cultural communication skills that do not rely on the old cultural mythology. Consult step 13 for what skills are needed.

18

Develop a Personal Vision of Eliminating Racism

Create a vision of what ending racism means to you.

Creating a personal vision of what eliminating racism means is an empowering tool that will support other steps you take. Your personal vision can express your hopes and desires about ending racism; it can also express your concerns and fears. Your personal vision about ending racism can take many forms—an affirmation, a prayer, a poem, a song, a painting, a ritual, or any other form of creative expression. Your personal vision statement need not be long, but it should come from your deepest feelings and convictions about ending racism. Your personal vision statement is something you can come back to again and again.

A SAMPLE PERSONAL VISION OF ENDING RACISM

I honor the oneness of humankind. In our different colors of skin I see a rainbow of humanity. In our different ways of life I feel a harmony of experience. In our different native tongues I hear a symphony of expression. In our different manners of faith I experience many paths to the Divine.

While I fully embrace my ethnic heritage, I wish not to be judged, or to judge others, by color of skin, way of life, native tongue, or faith. I have compassion for all who suffer under the ignorance and pain of racism and discrimination, and I commit myself to taking steps to bring this suffering to an end.

IDEAS FOR A PERSONAL VISION STATEMENT

- List the three most important reasons you have for eliminating racism. Now fashion these reasons into three paragraphs.
- Write a prayer about ending racism reflecting the religious and spiritual tradition you come from.
- Draw a picture of what it would be like to live without racism.
- Collect five stones of roughly the same size. Paint them different colors—red, black, yellow, brown, and white—representing our different skin colors.
- Collect and arrange five gems or crystals of different colors—red (rose quartz), black (obsidian), yellow (sulfur), brown (amber), and white (clear quartz)—representing the different skin colors of people throughout the world.
- Collect or draw the religious symbols of as many great religions as you can find.

STEPS YOU CAN TAKE

- Create your personal vision statement.
- Set aside a regular moment daily, weekly, or monthly to read or review your personal vision statement and reflect on its meaning.
- Change your personal vision statement as your awareness and actions toward eliminating racism change.
- If your personal vision statement is written or visual, display it somewhere you can read or see it frequently (a bathroom mirror, the refrigerator, a prominent place in your home).

FOR YOUR
FAMILY

19

Raising Children with Nonracist Beliefs

Consciously or unconsciously we pass along our values and beliefs to our children.

No one is born racist. By two years of age children notice skin-color differences, but until grade school that doesn't seem to matter—young children play and interact easily with other children of different ethnic backgrounds. Children become racist because of what they are taught directly, or indirectly, by adults. Racism is transmitted to children as much by what adults say and do, as it is by what is left unsaid and not done. Ultimately, racism cannot survive where difference and diversity are tolerated, accepted, welcomed, honored, and celebrated. Helping young children deal with diversity is the foundation of an antiracist upbringing. Diversity training begins within the family and ultimately extends to encompass others outside of the family. There are simple, gentle steps you can take to guide your children toward tolerance and acceptance, and steer them away from bias and bigotry. These may be the most important steps you take in your family toward ending racism.

DID YOU KNOW

- In a 1940s series of landmark studies by Kenneth and Mamie Clark on the effect of negative images of African Americans on children, 67% of black children chose white dolls to play with. The white dolls were perceived as more beautiful, acceptable, and desirable.
- In a 1988 study to recreate the Clarks' research, Derek Hopson and Darlene Powell-Hopson found that 65% of black children chose white dolls and 76% of these preschoolers said the black dolls "looked bad."
- After reading positive stories about black children, and repeating positive words about the dolls like *pretty, nice, clean,* and *smart,* the preschoolers in the 1988 study again got a chance to choose which doll to play with—68% then chose the black doll.

STEPS YOU CAN TAKE

- Demonstrate acceptance of your child's need to be separate and unique. Children will not learn to accept and tolerate difference in others if they have not experienced acceptance and tolerance for their differences. Help your child feel he or she lives in a family that respects and honors the uniqueness of each member. A classic study showed that children whose mothers demanded obedience grew up with more prejudicial beliefs than those whose mothers did not.
- Discuss ethnic differences. Children are fascinated with their bodies and the bodies of others. They are naturally attracted by people with different skin color, hair texture, and other different physical characteristics. Ignoring a discussion of human difference can lead children to feel uneasy about those differences; that something is wrong with people who are different from them.
- Celebrate diversity instead of color-blindness. Many baby boomers grew up with the idea of a color-blind, "melting-pot"

society—a popular post–World War II liberal notion in America. While it may seem noble to tell a child not to notice the differences in others—"It doesn't matter if a person is black, brown, or green"—it does, in fact, matter. Color-blindness is not a solution to racism. Diversity does not happen by neglect or default, it comes about by actively embracing difference. Help children find positive ways of incorporating human differences into their lives. For example, in response to a child noticing a person of color, you might say, "It's wonderful that so many different kinds of people live in our neighborhood. Each of us has something unique and special to offer the other."

- If your child comes home expressing prejudicial feelings, don't panic. He or she may be trying to cope with a new or unexpected situation that occurred at school or during play. Gently and consistently reinforce tolerant attitudes over racist attitudes: (1) acknowledge your child has some important feelings that need attention; (2) allow your child to express those feelings and talk about the situation that gave rise to them; (3) challenge any prejudicial feelings with counterexamples, additional information, or alternative interpretations; (4) play-act the situation that gave rise to your child's feelings. You take the role of your child and act out a response that reinforces tolerant attitudes and actions.
- Help your children learn how to handle prejudice. Inform them they have a right never to be subjected to racist slurs, or be present when racist remarks are directed at others. Play-act situations where this occurs and help them develop appropriate responses and behaviors: (1) telling a perpetrator, "I don't like what you're saying, please stop now"; (2) enlisting the support of a playmate or another adult; (3) reporting all incidents to some authority.
- Tell your children stories from your own life that help them deal with ethnic differences in positive ways.
- Screen the media (television, music, movies, videos, newspapers) and all other reading material your child is exposed to for attitudes about race and racism. If you are not satisfied with

what is presented, you can attempt to prohibit your child from being exposed to that material. This may not be as effective as spending time discussing your misgivings with your child, and reinforcing personal beliefs that counter what is portrayed in the media.

- Read your children stories that have positive images of people from all different ethnic groups.
- Expose your children to positive images of all ethnic groups from a very early age through dolls of different skin colors, toys from different cultures, reading material, music, educational videos, recreational and leisure activities.

REFERENCES

Edelman, Marian Wright. *The Measure of Our Success: A Letter to My Children and Yours*. Boston: Beacon Press, 1992. A thoughtful reflection by the executive director of the Children's Defense Fund.

Fitzpatrick, Jean Grasso, op. cit.

Hopson, Derek S., and Darlene Powell-Hopson. *Different and Wonderful: Raising Black Children in a Race-Conscious Society*. New York: Prentice-Hall Press, 1990.

Rochman, Hazel, ed. *Against Borders: Promoting Books for a Multicultural World*. Chicago: American Library Association, 1993.

RESOURCES

Children's Defense Fund, 25 E Street, NW, Washington, D.C. 20001. (202) 628-8787.

Council on Interracial Books for Children, 1841 Broadway, Rm. 608, New York, NY 10023.

Interracial Family Alliance, Box 16248, Houston, TX 77222. (713) 454-5018.

Interracial-Intercultural Pride, 1060 Tennessee St., San Francisco, CA 94107. (415) 399-9111.

National Coalition to End Racism in America's Child Care System, 22075 Koths, Taylor, MI 48180.

20

Know What Your Children Are Learning Outside the Home

Attitudes and beliefs about race and racism are inherited socially and culturally.

We are not born with beliefs about race and racism, we learn them as children from the social environment we live in. As parents interested in ending racism we must know what our children are learning about race and racism. We can make every effort to provide our children with an environment that honors the differences among ethnic groups, while embracing the fundamental wholeness of all humankind. Children need to feel good about the ethnic group they are part of, and good about the other ethnic groups they come in contact with.

Honoring difference while embracing wholeness begins in the family and extends to the schools, churches, civic organizations, and friends our children come in contact with. As parents our responsibility is to know what our children are learning, and what they are not learning, about race and racism. When we are uncomfortable with our children's education regarding race and racism, our responsibility is to step in and bring about change.

STEPS YOU CAN TAKE

- If your children are already in school, ask them what they know and believe about race and racism. Don't be surprised by their response, but don't be afraid to begin to correct any misperceptions your children harbor about race and racism.

- Find out how the curriculum in your children's school addresses questions of race and racism. Compare this curriculum against some of the suggestions in this book. If there are areas you feel are not addressed or are underaddressed, make an appointment to see a school official to voice your concerns.

- Determine what is being taught about race and racism through your children's religious education if they attend a Sunday school. Compare this with some of the suggestions in this book. If you are not comfortable with their religious education about race and racism, discuss your feelings with the pastor of the church or the director of their program or school.

- Have family discussions about race and racism. Say to children, especially when they are young, "What we as a family believe about [race, other ethnic groups, diversity, et cetera] is . . ."

- When your child gets older, involve him or her in a project that contributes to ending racism and promoting diversity.
  - Children at one elementary school were bothered by television advertisements for "flesh-colored" bandages when many of them were persons of color. They wrote letters to the manufacturer stating their concerns and convinced the advertiser to change the message.
  - PeaceNet (see step 15) has an electronic conference for kids only, which allows youngsters the world over to find pen pals and write to them through a home computer.
  - One parent left a message on the CompuServe computer network (see step 15) thanking Amnesty International for posting Urgent Appeals (see step 15). He used them to educate his children about human rights abuses throughout the world.

• Combine your efforts with those of other families working to instill antiracist values and beliefs in their children.

RESOURCES

The Activism 2000 Project for Kids was created to help young people engage in political and social projects that make a difference. The goals of the Activism 2000 are:

• to rekindle the spirit of idealism in young people
• to convert concern and compassion into action
• to link their energy with that of like-minded individuals
• to give them a taste of empowerment to pursue their vision
• to convince them that an individual can make a difference

The project publishes a book entitled *No Kidding Around,* which is filled with success stories about young people and their civic activism. It includes strategies for launching a successful project, and over a thousand resources for anyone working on concrete proposals for social, legal, and political change. The Activism Project 2000 states:

This mission goes far beyond convincing young Americans that democracy is not a spectator sport. The Activism 2000 Project wants to show people, including those who are not yet of voting age, how to play and how enormously rewarding it is to play. Political involvement at an early age has the potential for becoming a lifetime habit that spells hope for our aging democracy.

The Activism 2000 Project, P.O. Box E, Kensington, MD 20895. To order *No Kidding Around,* call (301) 929-8808, Fax: (301) 929-8907, (800) 955-POWER.

21

A Family Environment That Embraces Diversity

Make your home a model environment for celebrating diversity.

From our family we learn the values and beliefs that guide our actions and attitudes in the outside world. In our family life we have many opportunities to learn about and practice the acceptance of others who have different feelings, beliefs, and ideas. Our home, however humble, can be a symbol of commitment to the ideals of diversity and acceptance. From the pictures we hang on our walls, to the music we play on our stereos, to the way we celebrate holidays, our family and our home can be a model environment for embracing diversity and eliminating racism.

STEPS YOU CAN TAKE

- Decorate your home with artwork from different cultures and ethnic groups. Your local library or museum may have a lending collection of artwork you can choose from. This would allow you to rotate the art on a continual basis. The artwork you choose may evoke a discussion among members of your family. Use this as an opportunity to talk about the cultures from which the artwork comes. Use the artwork as a focal point for passing on beliefs and values about diversity and acceptance to your children.

- Obtain recordings of music from other cultures and ethnic groups. Your library may have a lending file of such recordings. Play the recordings for your family; discuss the people and culture from which the recordings come. Note the differences and similarities between music from different cultures and ethnic groups.
- Watch a videotape on some aspect of another ethnic group as a family and then discuss what you have seen. Your local library can provide you with many references to suitable videotapes.
- Enjoy an ethnic meal together and talk in positive ways about the people and culture the food comes from.
- Attend different religious services with your family (see step 24 for more information).
- Celebrate holidays of other ethnic groups (see step 22 for more information).
- Have your family become part of a foreign or domestic student exchange program. Speak to the counseling office or principal of the school your child now attends.

REFERENCES

Hayden, Carla D., ed. *Venture into Cultures: A Resource Book of Multicultural Materials and Programs.* Chicago: American Library Association, 1992.

RESOURCES

American Intercultural Student Exchange, 7720 Herschel Avenue, La Jolla, CA 92037. (619) 459-9761.

22

Honor the Holidays of Other Ethnic Groups

Honoring the special days of other ethnic groups is a family activity that celebrates diversity.

Every culture marks special days for celebration. To honor the holiday of another culture is to briefly immerse yourself and your family in the traditions of that culture, for these holidays are filled with spiritual, political, historical, and cultural significance. You will find similarities in the holidays celebrated by different cultures. Many holidays are clustered around the same time of year, or have similar themes. This happens because they were originally based upon common natural phenomena like the changing of the seasons, the honoring of birth and death, or the agricultural cycles of planting and harvesting. There is also much that is special and unique to each holiday: the accomplishments of an important historical figure; the recognition of an important event in the history of that culture; the wearing of special dress, or the preparation of special food. Honoring the holidays of other cultures is a particularly effective means of creating an environment for children that celebrates diversity and helps to eliminate racism.

MAJOR HOLIDAYS YOU CAN HONOR

CULTURE	NAME	DATE(S)	DESCRIPTION
African American	African American History Month	February	A month-long period to honor the history and contributions of African Americans.
African American	Martin Luther King, Jr., Day	Third Monday in January	An official holiday in the United States celebrating the life and accomplishments of this slain civil-rights leader.
African American	Kwanzaa	December 26– January 1	Celebrated by African Americans and people of African descent. Kwanzaa recognizes seven principles of community life: unity, self-determination, collective work, cooperative economics, purpose, creativity, and faith.
Islamic (Arabic)	Eid ul-Fitr, also known by other names such as Hari Raya Ruasa	During July	Celebrated at the end of Ramadan, a period of fasting. New clothing is worn, mosques are visited for prayers, and verses from the Quran are read for the ancestors.
Islamic (Arabic)	Eid ul-Adha	Tenth day of twelfth Islamic lunar month (usually in late spring or summer)	The festival of sacrifice commemorating Abraham's willingness to sacrifice his only son. A day where children wear new clothes and a lamb is sacrificed symbolically.
Chinese and Vietnamese	Chinese New Year Vietnamese Tet	First three days of first lunar month, in late January or early February	An important holiday with festivals, costumes, exchange of food and gifts.
Japanese	Oshogatsu Matsuri	January 1–3	Japanese New Year. New clothing is worn, the year is

			toasted with sake, children are given gifts, and Buddhist prayer bells ring out 108 times.
Japanese	O-Bon	July 10	Feast of Fortune, also a time of commemorating the ancestors.
Korean	Sol Day	First day of first lunar month, late January or early February	Celebrants dress in new clothes or traditional costumes. Kite flying is done to symbolize letting bad luck fly away.
Korean	Ch'usok	Fifteenth day of eighth lunar month, late September or early October	This is a harvest moon festival of thanksgiving where families gather for large feasts and visit the graves of their ancestors to give thanks.
Thai	Loy Krathong	Full moon of twelfth lunar month, in November or December	A festival of lights in which candles are floated along rivers and canals throughout the country.
Hindu	Dipavali, Divali, Diwali, or Dewali	Full moon of twelfth lunar month, in November or December	A festival of lights in which candles are placed around the house to welcome Lakshmi, the goddess of prosperity.
Hindu	Durga Puja	Full moon of eighth lunar month, September or October	A ten-day period set aside to honor the Divine Mother, as Goddess, as Nature, and as the sustainer of life.

Hispanic	Hispanic Awareness Month	September	A month-long period to honor the history and contribution of Hispanic Americans.
Hispanic	Cinco De Mayo	May 5	Celebrates Mexican desire to be free from foreign invaders, and defeat of the Emperor Maximilian's army in Mexico on May 5, 1867. Taken as a time for the celebration of Hispanic American culture.
Jewish	Rosh Hashanah	First day of Jewish lunar month Tishri, September or October	Jewish New Year with solemn prayers and the blowing of the shofar, a ram's horn.
Jewish	Hanukkah	Twenty-fifth day of Jewish lunar month Kislev, near Winter Solstice.	Festival of Lights celebrated for eight days and marked by the lighting of the eight candles of the menorah.
Native American	Native American Heritage Month	October	A month-long period to honor the history and contributions of Native Americans.

STEPS YOU CAN TAKE

- List additional holidays not included in the above chart. The major western holidays (Christmas, New Year's, Easter, et cetera) have not been shown in the above chart because they are so widespread and familiar. Many other holidays could be listed for the cultures shown in this chart, and for cultures and ethnic groups not shown. Contact local ethnic civic organizations for a list of other holidays important to their group.

• Read more about the background of these holidays; learn about their spiritual, political, and historical significance.
• Incorporate celebration of these holidays into that of holidays you already celebrate. Start with a holiday like Christmas and see how many holidays from other ethnic groups are close to it. Find some aspect of these other holidays that you can incorporate into Christmas. Make this an annual family tradition.
• Check among your friends to find those who may celebrate a particular ethnic holiday. Ask them to help you celebrate the holiday. Ask them where you might attend a holiday celebration. Invite them to your home to talk with your family about the meaning of the holiday for them.
• Write important ethnic holidays on a calendar that is displayed in a prominent location in your home. Include a brief description of the meaning and importance of each holiday.

RESOURCES

Coxfield, Carolyn. *My Kwanzaa Book.* Atlanta: Sea Island Information Group, 1990.

Hayden, Carla D., ed., op. cit. A wealth of material on celebrating different cultural holidays, with a good bibliography. Many of the holidays listed in the chart are explained and different methods for celebrating them are given. See resource section of step 22 for additional information.

King Center. *Official King Week Kit.* Atlanta: MLK, Jr., Center for Nonviolent Social Change, 1983.

National Education Association. *Martin Luther King, Jr.: A Guide to Observe the Birthday.* Washington: National Education Association, 1985.

The Software Toolworks. *Toolworks Desk Reference.* New York: Simon and Schuster, 1991.

Syracuse Cultural Workers, P.O. Box 6367, Syracuse, NY 13217, (315) 474-1132, publishes a calendar listing holidays from many different ethnic groups.

23

Discover Your Family's Ethnic Background

By accepting our own uniqueness we can accept the uniqueness of others.

All of us have unique ethnic backgrounds. One of the tragedies of modern life is the loss of this sense of uniqueness. We are led to believe in cultural ideals—"the American dream," "the American family," "the American melting pot," "the American way of life." Racism is an expression of intolerance for those who do not conform to these ideals, yet ironically few people do actually conform. In truth there are many American dreams, many American families, many different people in the same American pot, and many American ways of life.

Our tendency is to label ethnic groups. We believe in a "black culture," different from "white culture," different from "Hispanic culture." Once again this is a myth. There are many black cultures, many white cultures, many Hispanic cultures. For example, black culture in New Orleans is different from black culture in Harlem and both are different from black culture in rural Mississippi. White culture in Beverly Hills is different from white culture in Appalachia and both are different from white culture in a small midwest farming community.

Many of us are multicultural by birth. Our ethnic heritage is German, French, and Irish. Or it is African, Native American, and English. Or it is French, Native American, and Jewish. We are living examples of what it means to embrace unity in diversity. Learn to honor the uniqueness of your ethnicity, so you can honor the uniqueness of others'.

STEPS YOU CAN TAKE

- Create a family tree. Start by recalling the relatives you know, then ask those that are living to recall the relatives they know. When possible collect stories about your relatives.
- Organize a family reunion that brings together as many different branches of the family as possible.
- Find and interview your oldest living relatives. Ask them about their lives. Record the interview on video- or audiotape.
- Travel to the countries of origin of your relatives.
- Read about the history of the ethnic groups within your family's heritage.
- Discover the major holidays celebrated by the ethnic groups within your family's heritage (see step 22).
- How does your ethnic background affect who you are today? Your personality? Your life-style? Your interests?
- Consider what stereotypes of your ethnic background you would most like to release.
- Make a list of what you like most about your ethnic background.
- Involve your children in this investigation of family roots.
- Collect photographs of your ancestors. Ask family members for their photographs, have them copied, then create a framed display or album with a pictoral record of your family. Such pictoral family histories can be given as gifts during holidays.

RESOURCES

American Genealogical Research Institute. *How to Trace Your Family Tree: A Complete and Easy-to-Understand Guide for the Beginner.* Arlington, VA: American Genealogical Research, 1973.

Arnold, Jackie Smith. *Kinship: It's All Relative.* Baltimore: Genealogical Publishing Co., Inc., 1990.

Baer, F. M. *Creating a Family History.* Yakima, WA: Baer Publications, 1979.

Beard, Timothy Field, and Denise Demong. *How to Find Your Family Roots.* New York: McGraw-Hill Publishing Co., 1977.

Croom, Emily Anne. *Unpuzzling Your Past: A Basic Guide to Genealogy.* White Hall, VA: Betterway Publications, Inc., 1989.

Haley, Alex. *Roots.* Garden City, NY: Doubleday and Co., Inc., 1976.

Hook, J. N. *Family Names: The Origins, Meanings, Mutations, and History of More than 2,800 American Names.* New York: Macmillan Publishing Co., Inc., 1983.

Redford, Dorothy Spruill, and Michael D'Orso. *Somerset Homecoming: Recovering a Lost Heritage.* New York: Anchor Books, 1989. About tracing the history of a black family.

Rosenbluth, Vera. *Keeping Family Stories Alive: A Creative Guide to Taping Your Family Life and Lore.* Point Roberts, WA: Hartley & Marks, Inc., 1990.

24

Find Unity
in Spiritual Diversity

There are many roads to the same spiritual truth.

Racism and spirituality have an unfortunate and often violent relationship. The conflicting spiritual beliefs and practices of different ethnic groups are frequently the basis of hostility and warfare. Human history shows that more people have been killed in the name of God than for any other cause. Spirituality is also used to justify racism. One group reads into their scriptures reasons why they should discriminate against or subjugate another group. Christianity was used to justify the slavery and oppression of blacks in America. Protestantism is used to justify the oppression of Irish Catholics, Catholicism used to justify violence against English Protestants. Islam is used to justify the mistreatment of Jews, Judaism to justify poor treatment of Arabs. Hindus find a scriptural basis for violence against Sikhs, and Sikhs find spiritual support for warfare with Hindus. And the list of such conflicts goes on and on.

However, the spiritual teachings of all great religions do offer another way. Instead of finding a scriptural basis for separation and strife, we can find spiritual messages of the unity and oneness. Regardless of the nature of your spiritual beliefs you can look within those beliefs to find what joins you to the spiritual beliefs of other ethnic groups. You can also look within the spiritual beliefs of others to find what joins them to you. You can find unity in spirit amid the diversity of beliefs and practices. A family that finds this unity takes a step toward breaking down the artificial spiritual barriers that reinforce racism.

DID YOU KNOW

Light is a universal symbol of spirituality shared by all great traditions: the source of spirituality is frequently symbolized as light; the process of spirituality as movement toward that light; and the goal of spirituality as enlightenment itself. Light unites. The following quotes were taken from the inside of a temple in Buckingham, Virginia, built to honor the spiritual traditions of humankind:

- "In the lotus of the heart dwells Brahman the Light of lights." (Hinduism)
- "The Lord is my light; whom shall I fear?" (Judaism)
- "The Light of Divine Amaterasu shines forever." (Shinto)
- "Following the light, the sage takes care of all." (Taoism)
- "The radiance of Buddha shines ceaselessly." (Buddhism)
- "I have come into the world as light." (Christianity)
- "Allah is the Light of the heavens and the earth." (Islam)
- "God, being Truth, is the one Light of all." (Sikhism)
- "God is the sun beaming light everywhere." (Native African)
- "The light of Wakan-Tanka is upon my people." (Native American)

STEPS YOU CAN TAKE

- Visit the worship service of different ethnic groups with your family. This is often easier in a large city, where it is possible to find many different churches and places of worship. Most will be glad to welcome you among their worshipers. You may choose to participate as your own beliefs and comfort allow, or you can just observe. If the service is conducted in another language, ask someone to give you a brief explanation. Better yet, consult one of the listed references first to gain some understanding of what you'll witness. You might choose the service of a different ethnic group within your present faith, or that of a faith very different from yours. Regardless of where you go, allow yourself to experience the unity of spirit amid the diversity of beliefs. If we are united in spirit we cannot be divided by racism.

- Involve children in more than just the spiritual beliefs of other ethnic groups. One church in New York City had its Sunday school classes take a month to study each of the world's great religions. During that month they would attend a service of the selected religion, make the clothes worn by people of the culture from which the religion came, eat the food from the culture, and read about the spiritual and secular history of the people.

- Organize an "All Faiths Day" in your community. Invite local spiritual leaders reflecting all the different traditions in your community. If not enough are represented within your community, reach out to surrounding areas or the nearest large city. Invite local civic and political leaders, and invite the general public. Ask the spiritual leaders to speak on a theme like "Worshiping Unity Amid Our Diversity," then lead a short service from the spiritual tradition they represent.

- Honor the major religious holidays of other ethnic groups (see step 22).

- Invite a friend of another spiritual faith to your home to discuss his or her spiritual beliefs with your family.

REFERENCES

Ellwood, Robert S. *Many Peoples, Many Faiths: An Introduction to the Religious Life of Humankind.* Englewood Cliffs, NJ: Prentice-Hall Press, 1987.

Pelikan, Jaroslav Jan. _The World Treasury of Modern Religious Thought._ Boston: Little Brown and Co., 1990.

Vail, Albert R. and Emily M. _Transforming Light; the Living Heritage of World Religions._ New York: Harper & Row Publishers, Inc., 1970.

White, David Manning. _The Search for God._ New York: Macmillan Publishing Co., Inc., 1983. Over three thousand quotes from religions around the world.

RESOURCES

- The LOTUS (Light Of Truth Universal Shrine) temple is located in Buckingham, Virginia. It is a magnificent structure reminiscent of the Taj Mahal, built in the shape of a lotus flower. Under each large petal, within a central worship area, are altars to the world's great religions. For further information contact the Satchidananda Ashram, Route 1, Box 172, Buckingham, VA 23921, (804) 969-3121.

25

Develop
a Family Vision
of Eliminating Racism

Create a vision of ending racism that reflects the attitudes and beliefs you would like within your family.

A vision statement on ending racism is a gift to give your family. It is a way of communicating values and attitudes to your children, and a way of helping all family members understand that what happens in the world begins in the home. Just as with the personal vision statement (see step 18), the family vision statement can take many forms—an affirmation, a prayer, a poem, a song, a painting, a ritual, or some other form of creative expression. You may want to use more than one form of creative expression so all family members, regardless of age, can relate to the vision statement. Younger children, for example, might do better with a song or even a game. You can orchestrate the vision statement so that all family members contribute something to the final product.

A SAMPLE FAMILY VISION OF ENDING RACISM

Through this family's love we also love the greater human family. Each member of this family is a different, unique, and special human being. We honor the unity of our family's differences as we

99

honor our unity with people of different colors, customs, and spiritual faiths. As parents and adults in this family we act as models for how we hope our children will come to act in the world. We value the children of this family, for they are the future and the hope; as are children the future and hope the world over. In this family children are raised to believe in the equality of all men and women.

Our family believes that people should be valued for the content of their character rather than the color of their skin. We encourage each other to meet, work, play, live, and worship with people from all ethnic and cultural backgrounds. We feel that loving each other helps us better love our brothers and sisters regardless of skin color, way of life, or spiritual faith. Nurturing our family's love is a step we take toward eliminating the pain and despair of racism.

STEPS YOU CAN TAKE

- Create a family vision of ending racism with each family member contributing something to the vision statement. See step 18 for suggestions on the form the statement might take.
- Talk to children about the importance of the vision statement. Inform them they can talk to others about their family values and beliefs regarding racism.
- Revise the vision statement. Tell all family members they can continually add to the vision statement as their awareness and experience with ending racism changes.
- Display the family vision statement in a prominent location where all family members can see it (bathroom mirror, family room, refrigerator door).

FOR YOUR
COMMUNITY

26

Look Beneath
the Surface
of Your Community

Look beneath the surface of where you live to
discover what work there is to end racism.

It's easy to say, "The problem of racism is in New
York City, or Los Angeles, or San Francisco, or Atlanta, but it's not
here in my town." Look again, beneath the surface of your community. How well are the fundamental needs of all citizens being met—
physically, socially, economically, spiritually, and intellectually? Regardless of ethnicity, everyone in your community should have
these basic needs.

You may find that ethnicity plays a role in who gets these basic
needs and how well they are met. Where you find discrepancy or
disparity based on ethnicity is where you can work for changes that
will end racism.

TOOLS YOU CAN USE

NOTE: *You may wish to refer to the following tools throughout
the investigation of your community. They will be useful for the
next several items in this book.*

- A large map of your community. City hall or a local planning office can usually provide you with a planning map.
- 1990 census data for your community. This is available from the Government Printing Office in Washington, D.C. Be aware that federal census data may not be accurate for your purposes because ethnic minorities are often miscounted. Also check local sources of demographic information about your community: the state human relations commission, social service agencies, city planning departments, board of education, or community organizations.
- A list of the major firms, banks, colleges, and other institutions that do business in your community.
- A list of all local elected and appointed officials.
- A system for recording and maintaining the information you gather. Notebooks and file cards, or a simple computerized data base where you record information so it can be cross-referenced.

STEPS YOU CAN TAKE

- Determine who actually lives in your community. The demographic data you collect can help you determine the ethnic breakdown of your community in actual numbers and percentages. Such information can be helpful in identifying areas where changes can be made to help eliminate racism. For example, if the population of your community is 15% African American but only 4% of the administrative staff of a local hospital is African American, that might point to an area where improvement in employment practices can be made.
- If data are available about the geographic location of ethnic minorities in your community, shade in areas of your community where a high percentage of ethnic minorities live. This will also help you identify potential areas for improvement. Many covertly racist practices are tied in to geographic location. One study of racism in home insurance showed that callers to an insurance company were treated differently simply on the basis

of the street address they gave. See step 34 for more information on racism in housing. Other studies have shown that ethnic minority communities receive an unfair burden of toxic waste facilities (incinerators, waste dumps, factories with a high output of environmental pollutants). See step 48 for more information on environmental racism.

- Create a newspaper file of all articles and editorials related to racism and ethnicity. Don't stop with the local newspaper, but include high school and college papers, newsletters from local businesses, bulletins from social service agencies, and publications by local ethnic groups.

- Monitor local TV and radio stations (major networks, cable, high school, college, educational). Get program schedules to determine if they will be broadcasting programs that deal with racism and ethnicity.

- Make a synopsis of how well the local mass media addresses issues of racism and ethnicity. Some criteria would be: how many nonwhite reporters the media has relative to the nonwhite population of your community; how many stories are done about different local ethnic groups on a weekly or monthly basis; how supportive editorials are of equal participation by all local ethnic groups. Use a simple rating scale to evaluate newspapers, TV, and radio: 1 = not at all; 2 = somewhat; 3 = adequately; 4 = good; 5 = excellent.

- Visit different areas of your community. What obvious differences do you observe about the facilities and quality of life in different neighborhoods? Note and record the differences.

RESOURCES

Boice, Judith L. *The Art of Daily Activism*. Oakland, CA: Wingbow Press, 1992.

Heunefeld, John. *The Community Activist's Handbook: A Guide to Organizing, Financing and Publishing Community Campaigns*. Boston: Beacon Press, 1970.

Robbin, Peggy. *Saving the Neighborhood: You Can Fight Developers and Win*. Rockville, NY: Woodbine House, 1990.

YWCA. *Look Beneath the Surface of the Community*. New York: YWCA, 1974. This book specifically addresses community activism related to eliminating racism. It is a simple, straightforward handbook on the subject.

Zimmerman, Richard. *What Can I Do to Make a Difference?: A Positive Action Sourcebook*. New York: Penguin Books, 1991.

27

Understand Institutional Racism

Institutional racism is racism without a face.

Institutional racism is discrimination and unequal treatment by political, social, economic, and cultural institutions based on ethnicity. Unlike "hate crimes" there are usually no specific individuals responsible for acts of institutional racism. Institutional racism is a system of nearly invisible barriers based on ethnicity that prevent the movement of certain individuals into all areas of society.

Often, institutional racism is a reflection of the status quo. For instance, a social club may have no written policy against admitting persons of color or members of certain white ethnic groups. Yet in the one-hundred-year history of that social club there has never been a black or a Jew admitted.

Institutional racism is found in all segments of society. In order to comply with federal regulations a corporation may have to hire members of nonwhite ethnic groups. Yet after a twenty-year history of hiring minority workers few, if any, have made it to upper management positions although white workers with less seniority and experience have. This is often referred to as a "glass ceiling."

When two job applicants of equal background but different ethnicity apply for the same job or same home to rent, the white applicant is far more likely to succeed in obtaining the job or home than the ethnic minority.

Sports provides another example of institutional racism. Since the late 1940s major league baseball in America has included black players. In fact, blacks and other players of color now predominate in major league teams. Yet there are few persons of color in team management positions on the field or in the front office. A similar situation exists in other team sports like football and basketball, where blacks are valued as athletes but undervalued as coaches or managers.

Institutional racism affects lives, by affecting the opportunities granted to people. If a bank or insurance company "redlines" a given area of a city, businesses may not be able to get operating loans, or insurance premiums may be prohibitively high. If real estate agents "steer" business, only certain individuals will be shown dwellings for sale or rent in a particular area.

Usually there are nonracist explanations for institutional racism: "It's just the way things have been for years," "No one like that has ever applied," "It takes time to acquire the experience for a senior position," "There are not enough qualified minority applicants," "Our policy was based solely on economic considerations." Institutional racism is only invisible to those unaffected by it. If you take the time to look, you can see how it affects your life and the lives of others.

DID YOU KNOW

- Over 50% of the players in professional sports are ethnic minorities but minorities comprise less than 5% of the management positions in sports (president, general manager, chief financial officer, head of scouting, manager, or head coach).
- In Fortune 1000 companies less than 1% of top management positions are filled by ethnic minorities.
- Insurance premiums in South Los Angeles were so high, the

area was virtually "redlined." Following the riots in the King verdict many minority businesspeople—unable to purchase insurance previously—were unable to reopen their establishments.

- A recent study of mortgage applications revealed that blacks are twice as likely as whites to be rejected for a home loan.

28

Determine the Views of Community Leaders

Interview local leaders regarding racism in your community.

In any community there are a small number of individuals who set policies, a somewhat larger number who implement policies, a still larger number of individuals who comment on policies, and the vast majority who are affected by policies. This is the power structure of your community. It is composed of influential individuals in politics, law enforcement, banking, education, social services, real estate, industry, the arts, community organizations, and health care. Find out the views of these leaders regarding ways your community is working to end racism.

Smaller communities often afford opportunities to speak with local leaders in person. You may catch the mayor of your community walking down the street, or you might see the police chief at a local café. The children of a real estate company executive may play with your children. In a larger community or city you may need to write letters to these individuals, and read local editorial pages or news reports in order to learn their views on ending racism.

Your approach to these individuals, in person or by letter, can be very simple and straightforward. "Hello, my name is ———. I'm a citizen concerned with how our community addresses issues of racism and ethnic diversity. In your capacity as ——— could you tell me what is currently being done, and what plans your [organization, institution, office] has to address these important issues." Most leaders will gladly respond to your inquiry. By default, those who don't have also told you about their views on ending racism.

Remember to maintain a healthy objectivity in listening to the responses of local leaders. One goal you should have is to evaluate what is being said about efforts to end racism with what is actually being done. Record the responses of these leaders in the file you are keeping on ending racism in your community.

INTERVIEWS YOU CAN CONDUCT

- Mayor
- Members of the city council
- Chief of police
- City attorney
- Presidents of the largest banks
- College presidents
- School principals
- Heads of largest real estate companies
- Heads of largest local industries
- Director of public health
- Director of arts council
- Leaders of community organizations
- Editors of local newspapers

29

Evaluating
an Institution

Discover whether the practices of a given
company or organization contribute to ending
racism.

Before you invest in, work for, join, or buy the
products of a company or organization you may want to know
about its practices with regard to institutional racism. There are
some major institutional vital signs that can help you out. Each vital
sign will educate you as to attitudes and practices that either encourage or discourage the inclusion of individuals from diverse ethnic groups.

When evaluating an institution you can write to the corporate
headquarters, or ask pertinent questions in person (when applying
for a job or a loan, for example). Remember to have an objective
viewpoint when assessing an institution's responses to your inqui-
ries. Focus on what an institution has actually done, compared to
the goals and plans an institution has to end racism.

INSTITUTIONAL VITAL SIGNS TO ASSESS[1]

- *Board of Directors:* Who sits on the board? What are their
  social, political, cultural, ethnic affiliations?

- *Employment:* Ethnic composition of the job force throughout the organization. Recruitment, outreach, and retention policies. Fairness of the application and interviewing process. Fair salary levels across ethnic groups. Equal opportunity for promotions. In-house training programs on discrimination and diversity. In-house counseling for problems of prejudice. Attitudes of persons with the ultimate decision on hiring. Equal access to employee benefits.
- *Services and Suppliers:* Ethnic composition of the independent professionals and subcontractors used by the organization: doctors, lawyers, accountants, janitorial, office supplies, banking, insurance, food service, et cetera.
- *Investments:* Property owned by the institution. Location. Financial portfolio managed by whom? Nature and composition of stockholders. Does the company invest in a socially conscious way? (See step 14 for more information.)
- *Advertising:* Firm employed. Models employed by ethnicity. Image projected by ad campaigns. Media used. Communities reached. Images of ethnic groups portrayed in ads.
- *Government:* Involvement of the federal government through funding or contracts. Compliance with government regulations regarding workplace discrimination, equal opportunity, and affirmative action.
- *Merchandising:* Percentage of credit accounts across ethnic groups. Involvement of minorities in credit granting. Ethnic composition of the sales force.
- *Unions:* Does one exist? Who belongs? What are the recruitment policies? Are union leaders representative of the ethnic composition of the work force?
- *Contributions:* Are contributions made to organizations working to eliminate racism?
- *Commitment to Diversity:* Company programs to eliminate racism in the workplace. Programs to encourage a more ethnically diverse work force. Tolerance, sensitivity, and diversity training programs for company workers. Grievance procedures.

- *Overall Image:* What overall image of the company is created through pictures in stores, headquarters, bulletin boards, menus?

REFERENCES

[1]Adapted from "Inventory of Racism: How to Look for Institutional Racism," found in Robert E. Terry, *For Whites Only* (Grand Rapids, MI: Wm. B. Eerdsmans Publishing Co., 1970), pp. 101–104.

Katz, Judith, op. cit.

Boice, Judith L., op. cit.

Heunefeld, John, op. cit.

Robbin, Peggy, op. cit.

YWCA, op. cit.

Zimmerman, Richard, op. cit.

30

Eliminating Racism in Education

Education is a basic tool in ending racism.

Along with jobs, education ranks high on the list of basic needs that are important in ending racism in your community. Education can correct the misinformation that accompanies racism; education can highlight contributions of many ethnic groups to the country and community you live in; but most importantly education provides training for the work force of tomorrow, and a way of escaping the cycles of poverty and injustice that accompany racism.

Content and curriculum are not the only indicators of educational quality. Policy making, community and parental involvement, student performance, and adult education are some other aspects to consider as well.

DID YOU KNOW

- In 1977 51% of all white high school students went on to college, as did 50% of all black high school students.
- In 1986 56% of all white high school students went on to college, while only 37% of all black high school students did.

QUESTIONS YOU CAN ASK

- Who is on the educational governing or policy-making board(s) by age, ethnic group, and sex? What are their feelings about racism and ethnicity in your community and in education?
- Do all ethnic groups in your community have a representative voice in educational policy-making?
- What is the ethnic composition of educational program administrators?
- Do both private and public educational systems exist in your community? How do they compare?
- Where are public and private school buildings located? What is their condition?
- How many people are employed by the schools in your community? Do they reflect the ethnic composition of the community? In teaching positions? In administrative positions? In counseling positions?
- What is the ratio of teachers to counselors? What kind of counseling is available? Is peer group counseling available?
- What training do teachers and counselors regularly receive regarding the life-styles of young people, ethnic and sexual differences, the job market, college entrance?
- Are there special education programs for the handicapped, mentally retarded, pregnant teens, unmarried mothers, and school dropouts?
- What is the ethnic composition of the student population in your community?
- Are public or private schools in your community de facto segregated?
- What are the average classroom sizes in different grades?
- What are the reading and mathematics scores of students—by age, ethnicity, and sex?
- What percentage of high school graduates go on to college—by age, ethnicity, and sex?
- Does the school have a curriculum that features contributions made by members of all ethnic groups?

- Is there an active, effective parent-teacher association in the schools?
- In what ways are parents encouraged to make input into the educational system?
- Are there adequate and accessible nursery schools, kindergartens, and child-care centers in your community? Under what auspices are they run?
- Are the latest government programs being utilized by schools in your community?
- Is there a lunch, and possibly a breakfast, program in your school system?
- Is school transportation readily available to all students who need it?
- Are adult education programs available through the school system? Do they include high school equivalency (GED) and English as a Second Language (ESL)?
- What institutions of higher education exist in your community? Universities? Colleges? Community Colleges? Junior Colleges? Vocational training school?
- What is the student population of these institutions by ethnicity?
- Are higher education scholarships available, and if so to whom?
- Do the institutions of higher education have plans for attracting and retaining students from diverse ethnic groups?
- How ethnically diverse are the faculty and administrative staffs of the institutions of higher education in your community?

STEPS YOU CAN TAKE

- Talk about your views on racism and the need to ensure ethnic diversity in your community's education institutions. Talk to educational policy-makers, school administrator, teachers, students, and other parents.
- Obtain copies of course catalogs and brochures from educational institutions.

- Attend school classes.
- Attend meetings of the local school board. Voice your opinions about curricula, hiring decisions, and other issues related to ending racism.
- Approach the president of a local college or the head of a local school board about starting a minority community advisory committee to work with the school on matters of racism and ethnic diversity.

RESOURCES

Boice, Judith L., op. cit.
Heunefeld, John, op. cit.
Robbin, Peggy, op. cit.
YWCA, op. cit.
Zimmerman, Richard, op. cit.

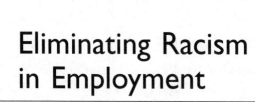

31

Eliminating Racism in Employment

Determine how easy it is for people of all ethnic backgrounds to find work in your community.

Jobs are the economic basis of every community. Without jobs people have little hope in their lives. The unemployment rate among ethnic minorities is nearly twice as high as the rate among white Americans. Disproportionate unemployment and underemployment among ethnic minorities is a sign of institutional racism. In your community, find out where the jobs are, what the jobs are, and who has them.

DID YOU KNOW

- By the year 2000 85% of America's work force will be women and members of ethnic minorities.
- A Los Angeles employment firm, Interplace, used code words to disguise its racist hiring practices. When an employer called seeking a new employee:
  - "Talk to Maria" actually meant "I prefer Hispanics."
  - "See me" actually meant "No people of color."

- "Talk to Mary" actually meant "I prefer Caucasians."
- "No Z" actually meant "No blacks."

STEPS YOU CAN TAKE

- Find out what kinds of jobs are in your community. Consult the local Better Business Bureau, the local chamber of commerce, the planning and development office, the nearest office of the state employment commission.
- Use your community map to locate and mark these places of employment.
- Determine the composition of the work force in your community by age, ethnic group, sex, and job skills. You may need to check with the equal employment opportunity officer of the major employers in your community, the state employment commission, or the state human relations commission.
- Determine the unemployment rate in your city for the total population and for different ethnic groups. Is there disparity in this rate?
- Ascertain what programs major local employers have in place to attract and retain minorities in their firms. Speak with the companies' personnel departments, the state employment commission, or the state human rights commission. What have their track records been to date?
- Find out what labor unions exist in your community. Use the yellow pages, a call to city hall, or contact the state labor commission.
- Determine what type of impact the labor unions have on the community. You may know this from having lived in the community for a long time. You can also check newspaper editorials and letters to the editor, and you can ask workers who you know belong to the unions.
- Find out the ethnic composition of local labor unions. Are the unions ethnically exclusive or does their membership reflect the diversity with your community?

- Determine if people of color have leadership positions in local unions.
- Do local unions have educational programs on racism and diversity for new members?
- Volunteer as an employment tester. This will involve being given an educational background and resume similar to another person of different ethnicity. You will both receive training from the agency conducting the investigation, then you will both apply for the same job, or register with the same employment service. The nature of the treatment received by you and your counterpart will assist in the monitoring of racism in employment within your community. Contact your state department of labor or a local legal or civil rights organization to get more information about being an employment tester.
- Organize a jobs fair in your community where local employers send representatives to talk to prospective employees with a special emphasis on employees of different ethnic minorities. A jobs fair can take place at many different levels. As early as grade school a jobs fair can stimulate the interest of young children to secure the education that will help them obtain a satisfying, financially rewarding job. For high school students a jobs fair might motivate them to go on to college. For college graduates a jobs fair can help identify what jobs exist. For older workers a jobs fair can help them secure employment or discover what additional training they may need to make themselves more employable. Contact your state or local department of employment or other civic organizations about sponsoring a jobs fair to help eliminate racism.
- See step 42 for additional information on discrimination in employment.

REFERENCES

Boice, Judith L., op. cit.
Heunefeld, John, op. cit.
Robbin, Peggy, op. cit.
YWCA, op. cit.
Zimmerman, Richard, op. cit.

32

Eliminating Racism in Agriculture

Agriculture brings together people from different ethnic groups.

If your community has a strong agricultural sector, investigate the relationship between farmers, workers, and labor unions. Frequently agriculture employs migrant laborers who come from specific ethnic groups. Often these workers are not well educated and do not have a good command of English. You should be interested in the treatment of migrant laborers, the extent to which they are able to exercise their rights, their access to education, and the extent to which they are supported by a union.

QUESTIONS YOU CAN ASK

- To what extent is the economy of your community dependent on agriculture?
- What kind of agriculture exists in your community—dairy, trucking, gardening, specialized?
- How many persons are employed in agriculture?
- Are migrant workers employed? Where do they come from?

- What are the wages of migrant laborers as compared to other farm workers?
- Where and how do tenant farmers and migrants live?
- What school and child-care facilities exist for migrant workers?
- What health care facilities exist for migrant workers?
- To what organizations do local farmers belong?
- Are migrant workers organized in unions?
- Are there current boycotts of farm products such as grapes or lettuce? Why? Which groups are observing the boycotts?
- Do migrant workers have full access to government programs and agricultural organizations?
- What government agency set labor standards for local migrant workers?
- What is the history and current relationship between local farmers and migrant workers?

STEPS YOU CAN TAKE

- Support the ongoing boycott of California table grapes by the United Farm Workers. Pesticides used in the production of these grapes have caused birth defects in migrant farm workers. Buy grapes, and other agricultural products, supported by the United Farm Workers and other migrant labor groups.
- Talk with local farmers about their relationship with migrant workers of different ethnic groups.
- Talk with migrant workers about their treatment and working conditions.
- Talk with farm labor union organizers and farm-worker community leaders about the problems that exist for local migrant workers.
- Visit migrant worker housing.
- Volunteer as an ESL (English as a Second Language) tutor or teacher. Contact your state or local department of education, and department of employment about ESL programs.
- Attend meetings about the issues facing the farm industry and migrant workers in your community.

• Join an organization that champions the conditions of migrant workers.

REFERENCES

Boice, Judith L., op. cit.
Heunefeld, John, op. cit.
Robbin, Peggy, op. cit.
YWCA, op. cit.
Zimmerman, Richard, op. cit.

ADDITIONAL RESOURCES

United Farm Workers, Box 62, La Paz, Keene, CA 93531. (805) 822-5571. A free videotape is available from UFW, *No Grapes,* that documents the reasons behind their grape boycott.

33

Eliminating Racism in Health Care

The health of a community is reflected in how that community cares for the health of its citizens.

Access to adequate health care is a fundamental need of all people. The high cost of health care, and the high cost of medical insurance premiums often places basic health care out of the reach of many citizens. Unfortunately these citizens are disproportionately members of ethnic minorities, and the health care system thus becomes another area where institutionalized racism is prevalent.

DID YOU KNOW

- Hypertension strikes twice as many black as whites. A 1991 study showed that anger over racism was a risk factor in high blood pressure.
- A study by the federal government showed that blacks and other ethnic minorities were less likely to receive adequate care at the nation's health care facilities.
- Infant mortality among blacks is more than twice as high as that among whites.

- Low-birth-weight babies are twice as likely among blacks than whites.
- Prenatal health care only late in pregnancy is twice as likely among blacks than among whites.
- The rate of HIV infection in the general population is decreasing in all population groups except blacks in urban areas.
- A man living in Bangladesh has a higher life expectancy than an African American male living in Harlem.
- A baby born in Cuba has a higher likelihood of survival than a baby born in Washington, D.C.

QUESTIONS YOU CAN ASK

- What health care facilities exist in your community and where are they located?
- Where is the nearest public health facility?
- Does the staff of local health care facilities (administrators and care-givers) reflect the ethnic composition of the community?
- Do local health care facilities have a community relations program? If so, does it serve all ethnic groups within your community?
- What local chapters of national health agencies (Planned Parenthood, American Cancer Society, Heart and Lung Association, and so on) exist in your community, and what services do they provide?
- Do local health care facilities understand and respect the traditional healing practices of different ethnic groups within your community?
- How many people within your community are without a basic health-insurance policy—by ethnicity, age, and sex?
- How do local hospitals handle patients without insurance, or patients who are underinsured?
- How are Medicare and Medicaid programs administered in your community?
- Are the hospitals in your community de facto segregated? For

instance, do some hospitals have a disproportionate number of low-income and ethnic-minority patients?

- Does your community have access to alternate health care providers (chiropractors, acupuncturists, massage therapists, et cetera)? Do these practitioners serve patients from all ethnic groups?
- What health outreach programs exist for members of all ethnic groups regarding AIDS, smoking, substance abuse, teen pregnancy, prenatal care, veterans, and family planning?
- Is health care information available in languages other than English?
- What is the infant mortality rate of white and nonwhite babies within your community?
- What mental health services exist within your community?

STEPS YOU CAN TAKE

- Find out from leaders of local ethnic organizations if special health care problems exist.
- Determine if overlapping problems exist in health care (e.g., toxic waste dumps located in low-income or ethnic minority communities, ambulance companies refusing to serve minority communities).
- Volunteer at a local health care facility serving all ethnic groups within your community.
- Organize a health fair that makes a special outreach to members of minority ethnic groups. This could be as simple as a blood pressure screening clinic or it could involve local health care agencies (hospitals, private practitioners, health educators) in a more comprehensive one-day program of education, assessment, and health care delivery.

REFERENCES

Kleg, Michael J., et al. "The Association of Skin Color with Blood Pressure in U.S. Blacks with Low Socioeconomic Status." *Journal of the American Medical Association* (February 6, 1991).

Sullivan, Louis W. (then secretary of health and human services), "Effects of Discrimination and Racism on Access to Health Care." *Journal of the American Medical Association* (November 20, 1991).

Boice, Judith L., op. cit.

Heunefeld, John, op. cit.

Robbin, Peggy, op. cit.

YWCA, op. cit.

Zimmerman, Richard, op. cit.

34

Eliminating Racism in Housing

Evaluate how adequately the housing needs of all citizens in your community are being met.

Housing is a basic need of all people. Although federal, state, and local ordinances mandate the practice of fair housing, ethnic minorities frequently encounter racism in the housing market. Racism in housing can take any number of forms. Potential home buyers will only be shown homes in certain locations—a practice called *steering*. A black couple who qualify to buy a house in any area of the community will only be shown houses in areas where other black families live. They will not be informed of houses in exclusively white neighborhoods. Similarly, renters will not be shown available apartments and homes because of their ethnicity.

In one southern city, realtors servicing a growing Vietnamese population decided to "steer" potential home renters to one area of the city. This practice effectively created an upscale ghetto, derisively dubbed "Little Saigon," identified exclusively with one ethnic group. Similar practices occur with low-cost and public housing in which different ethnic groups are "steered" to certain housing facilities, and ethnically homogeneous enclaves are thus created.

Another common racist housing practice is double-standard qualification. Two couples, one black the other white, apply for the same rental home. Both couples have the same educational background, the same joint salary, and the same credit rating. The black couple apply first and are either told they do not qualify, or that no rental units are available. But the white couple who apply immediately afterward are told they qualify and shown available housing.

Redlining is yet another racist housing practice. In this case banks and lending institutions exclude certain areas of the city from mortgages because of the ethnicity of the residents; the tolerance of substandard housing conditions and slum landlords for ethnic minorities; the location of low-cost or public housing in hazardous areas; and lack of adequate procedures for handling complaints of unfair housing practices.

QUESTIONS YOU CAN ASK

The following questions can be directed to the local real estate board, your civic planning authority, members of the city council, the mayor, or your state's commission on human rights. You can also obtain answers from scanning local newspapers, or asking local civic organizations.

- How many housing units exist in your community—single family, multiple units, public, private?
- What is the ethnic composition of the residential population of public housing units?
- What are the selection and eviction criteria for residents of public housing units?
- Are there associations for protecting tenants' rights?
- Is there a shortage of housing for any ethnic group?
- What areas of the community are zoned as residential? Are certain ethnic groups predominant in given residential areas?
- Does slum housing exist in your community? Where are the slums? Who are the slum landlords?

- What is the average cost of rental housing in your community —rooms, apartments, single-family houses?
- What is the average cost of purchasing a new home? An existing home?
- Do local banks make mortgages available in all areas of your community?
- Are there open- or fair-housing ordinances in your community? How are they enforced? What grievance and appeal procedures exist? What is the position of the local real-estate board and the local apartment owners' association on open/ fair housing?

STEPS YOU CAN TAKE

- Volunteer as a housing tester. As a tester you will be asked to play the role of a person interested in renting or buying housing. You will receive training along with other people who have volunteered as housing testers. The response you receive from a real estate agent or landlord will be compared against their responses to other housing testers to determine if discriminatory housing practices exist. Contact the human rights commission in your state, or a civil rights organization like the NAACP, for information about volunteering to be a housing tester. See step 44 for a list of such organizations.
- Carefully choose the area you rent or buy in. Even though you may not be a member of an ethnic minority that is discriminated against in housing, you may not want to live in an area that has been targeted to keep minorities out. Find out about the ethnic composition of an area before you purchase your home. Ask questions of your realtor before making a decision where to buy.
- Volunteer as a member of an organization working to build or create affordable housing like Habitats for Humanity.
- Volunteer with local groups attempting to buy back and renovate slum housing.

- Attend public meetings on property rights, real estate zoning, and housing. Evaluate the positions of elected officials, community agencies, and private individuals in light of housing and its affect on racism within your community.

REFERENCES

Boice, Judith L., op. cit.
Heunefeld, John, op. cit.
Robbin, Peggy, op. cit.
YWCA, op. cit.

35

Eliminate Racism in Justice and Law Enforcement

Law enforcement and justice are two areas where racism in a community is often most visible.

W̲ho can forget the brutal beating of Rodney King by Los Angeles police officers or the violent aftermath of the jury verdict in this case? Law enforcement and justice are two areas where racism is often visible and frequently tragic. Shortly after the King verdict, Amnesty International released a report on law enforcement in Los Angeles. The study, which had taken many months to compile, cited Los Angeles law enforcement with violations of human rights that would not be tolerated in other countries of the world. The target of these human rights abuses: primarily people of color. Not all police departments have a record like this, but you can learn a lot about racism in your community by investigating the fields of justice and law enforcement.

QUESTIONS YOU CAN ASK

You can ask these questions of law enforcement officials such as the chief of police, the mayor or chairman of the city council, the head of the state police, the state attorney general's office, the state human rights commission. You can also ask local civic organizations whose members may have had direct experience with law enforcement practices in your community.

- What law enforcement agencies operate in your community (police department, sheriff's department, federal marshal's office, city attorney's office, et cetera)?
- Does the staff of all law enforcement and justice agencies reflect the ethnic composition of your community (administrators and officers)?
- Have there been cases where law enforcement has been charged with excessive use of force?
- Are there different standards of enforcement for high-income citizens when compared to young people, low-income people, and members of ethnic minorities? You can get some feeling for fairness in law enforcement by:
  - Looking at arrest records and finding the number of ethnic minorities housed in your local jail
  - Asking law enforcement authorities about what communities have neighborhood Crime Watch programs
  - Finding out how patrol cars, beat police officers, and other law enforcement resources are distributed throughout your community
  - Questioning local ethnic minority civic organizations about information they have on fairness in law enforcement
- Does the police department have a community relations program? How is this program different in predominantly white areas as opposed to nonwhite areas of the community?
- What training do police officers receive in community relations? In dealing with members of different ethnic groups?
- Is there a citizens' review board for police activities?
- Is there a citizens' patrol within all areas of your community?
- What legal services are available in your community?
- Is legal representation available to all citizens regardless of income, ethnicity, sex, or age?

- Are members of all ethnic groups in your community available as potential jurors in civil and criminal cases?
- Who is imprisoned in your community—by income, ethnicity, sex, and age?
- What are the conditions within your community's prisons?
- Are rehabilitation, education, and work-release programs available in community detention facilities?
- What is the rate of recidivism (return to jail after serving a sentence)?
- Who are the judges, lawyers, and members of the parole board within your community?

STEPS YOU CAN TAKE

- Attend a meeting of the police-community relations board or committee.
- Meet whoever in the local police department is responsible for community relations.
- Form a police-community relations board if one does not exist.
- Form a police review board composed of community officials and local citizens, if one does not exist.
- Make sure you are asked to serve on jury duty.
- Volunteer at a community legal services agency.
- If you see law enforcement officers engaged in questionable activity, report what you've seen to an appropriate state or local agency like the state human-relations commission, or a local police review board.

RESOURCES

The Civil Rights Act of 1964 established the U.S. Department of Justice's Community Relations Service (CRS). The CRS operates a twenty-four-hour, toll-free number for anyone seeking assistance with regard to conflicts based on race, color, or national origin. Call the CRS hotline at 1-800-347-HATE, if:

- You have witnessed, have been victimized by, or have information about a community conflict based on race, color, or national origin.
- You are aware of racial tension that is rising in your community and believe racial violence may occur.

REFERENCES

Boice, Judith L., op. cit.
Heunefeld, John, op. cit.
Robbin, Peggy, op. cit.
YWCA, op. cit.
Zimmerman, Richard, op. cit.

36

Utilize the Arts

Evaluate the contribution the arts make toward ending racism in your community.

The arts are a central and defining part of any culture. They are one of the few aspects of a minority culture that often survive racism and oppression. For example, despite more than two centuries of slavery in America, African art survived among Africans held in captivity. African forms of music and dance are very much in evidence today as jazz, soul, blues, rhythm and blues, rap music, and rock 'n' roll. As a form of communication and self-expression art builds good will. It is also an excellent way to learn more about another ethnic group's history and culture.

QUESTIONS YOU CAN ASK

- Is there a local arts council? Who sits on the council? Is it representative of the ethnic diversity of the community? Is there a commitment to supporting projects reflective of diverse ethnic background?
- What local theater groups are there? Where are they located?

Are some dedicated to the interests of specific ethnic groups or social issues?

- What other local arts centers exists—galleries, coffeehouses, jazz clubs, art associations? Who are the members? Who are the organizers? Who are the artists found in these centers? Are they representative of a diverse ethnic background?
- What local dance and music groups exist (ballet companies, ethnic dance companies, orchestras, bands)?
- Is there a local museum(s)? Who sits on the board? Are museum exhibits reflective of diverse ethnic backgrounds?
- If there is a local university, college, junior college, or community college, does it have art, drama, film, music, and dance departments that are accessible to the community? Does the institution sponsor arts programs representative of diverse ethnic backgrounds?
- Are there local arts programs specifically for children? Do they expose children to arts from diverse ethnic backgrounds?
- Does the local newspaper include a calendar listing for arts programs from all the ethnic groups represented in your community?

STEPS YOU CAN TAKE

- Attend local arts programs, especially those of different ethnic groups. Take your children to expose them to art, dance, music, theater, and film from diverse backgrounds.
- Join the board of a local arts council, group, or institution. Voice your opinion about the wisdom of bringing arts from diverse ethnic backgrounds into your community.
- Organize a multicultural crafts fair. Invite members of different ethnic groups to present art forms unique to their ethnic heritage.
- Organize a multicultural music festival.
- Organize a local performance for a favorite performing artist or company whose work speaks to ending racism.

RESOURCES

Boice, Judith L., op. cit.
Heunefeld, John, op. cit.
Robbin, Peggy, op. cit.
YWCA, op. cit.
Zimmerman, Richard, op. cit.

37

Evaluating
Different Aspects
of Your Community

Any aspect of your community can be evaluated in terms of its impact on eliminating racism.

So it's been suggested that you evaluate many important aspects of your community in terms of their impact on eliminating racism—education, employment, agriculture, housing, law enforcement and justice, and the arts. But there are other equally important aspects of community life where you can work to eliminate racism—sports and recreation, public works (water, sewage, solid waste management, recycling), community administration, planning, and community development. In fact any aspect of your community can be evaluated in terms of how it attempts to eliminate racism. You go about this first by asking the right questions, then by formulating a plan for eliminating the discrepancies and inequities your questions uncover.

QUESTIONS YOU CAN ASK

- Who's in charge of this aspect of your community? Do those in charge reflect the ethnic composition of your community?
- Is there a mechanism in place to incorporate the views and

ideas of diverse ethnic groups into the policy-making process of this aspect of your community?

- What problems do community leaders and civic groups identify in this area of your community? What plans are in place to address these problems?
- Is there a history of racism in this aspect of your community? You may need to check local newspapers back several decades to find answers to these questions.
- How do members of your community find out about the services provided?
- What facilities are used for service delivery? Where are these facilities located? Is there easy access by all members of your community to these facilities?
- How does this aspect of your community measure its performance? Does this measure address eliminating racism or promoting diversity? If so, how does this aspect of your community measure up?

38 Make Martin Luther King, Jr., Day a Celebration of Diversity

Martin Luther King, Jr., Day is a fitting day to celebrate diversity and acknowledge the steps taken toward eliminating racism in your community.

America does not have a national holiday that honors diversity and steps taken toward eliminating racism, but there is no more fitting day to do this than the third Monday of January, the national holiday to commemorate Dr. Martin Luther King, Jr. More than any other figure in modern America, Dr. King worked tirelessly and gave his life in the struggle for freedom, justice, and equality for all Americans. Why not make Martin Luther King, Jr., Day a day your community honors the ideals represented by this Nobel laureate and dynamic leader in the movement to end racism?

WHAT KING SAID

"Even though we face the difficulties of today and tomorrow, I still have a dream. It is a dream deeply rooted in the American dream. I have a dream, that one day this nation will rise up and live out the true meaning of its creed, 'We hold these truths to be self-evident that all men are created equal.' I have a dream that one day on the red hills of Georgia, the sons of former slaves and the sons of former slave owners will be able to sit down together at the table of brotherhood. . . . I have a dream that my four little children will one day live in a nation where they will not be judged by the color of their skin but by the content of their character."—Martin Luther King, Jr., the March on Washington, August 1963.

STEPS YOU CAN TAKE

- Ask the mayor or city council to issue a proclamation declaring Martin Luther King, Jr., Day a day your community will officially acknowledge the ideals of brotherhood, equality, and acceptance advocated by Dr. King.
- If your community government does not officially recognize this day as a holiday, organize a citizens' group to request this day become an official holiday.
- Contact local churches and synagogues, asking them to incorporate the theme of racial harmony and the elimination of racism into the sabbath service before the holiday.
- Contact your community school board and ask that children throughout the public school system be given educational material that addresses Dr. King's life, the need to eliminate racism, and the importance of diversity.
- Contact local news media with your plans for the day.
- Plan a civic event that commemorates Dr. King and addresses the need to continue his fight against racism locally. Work with the civic organizations of African Americans and others interested in this civic event. Invite speakers from different ethnic groups. Invite political leaders to speak. Invite cultural groups to perform. Make this an annual event.
- See step 22 for additional information and resources regarding this holiday.

39

Organize a Civic Event

You don't have to rely on someone else to implement an idea about ending racism.

From a protest march to a crafts fair, you can learn to put on a successful civic event that makes a difference in the life of your community and contributes to ending racism. Civic organizing isn't hard; in fact it is the lifeblood of participatory democracy. In organizing your event you'll learn a lot about the community you live in. Afterward you'll be looked upon as a person whose ideas count, someone whom others turn to for opinions and for getting things done. Make your civic event part of a long-range plan you've developed to eliminate racism in your community.

STEPS FOR ORGANIZING A CIVIC EVENT

1 Choose a theme. If you're implementing one of the civic ideas in this book, the theme can be taken right from the text.
2 Write a brief statement of your goals in organizing this event. For example: "I'd like to organize an All Faiths Day in Bayview to celebrate the ethnic and spiritual diversity of this community."

3 Select an appropriate date. The date should not conflict with other major events. It might be best chosen around a related holiday or time of the year. Give yourself plenty of lead time to organize the event.

4 Select an appropriate location.

5 Write out the schedule for the day. If the event starts at one P.M. and ends at five P.M., make a list of everything that will happen from the point of view of a person attending.

6 Make a list of the special invited guests: speakers, political and civic leaders, civic organizations.

7 Make a list of all the supportive material and equipment you will need for activities: booths, name tags, microphones, speakers, public address system, music system, electrical hookups. Anything you can think of.

8 Make a budget based on the above list—include rental fees, speaker honorarium, support personnel—and the estimated fees, if any, you'll be collecting from those in attendance.

9 If you need funding determine likely funding sources. Consider local businesses, a local college, civic organizations, or private citizens who are sympathetic to the goals of your event.

10 Get media coverage of your event. Do not wait until the last minute to start arranging media coverage. Write a press release about the event. This is a short, succinct statement describing the goals and detailing when, where, and why the event is taking place. Distribute the press release to local TV, radio, and newspapers. Follow up with calls to these institutions. Tell them you're available for interviews.

11 Get word of the event out to the general public. Flyers, posters, and advertisements are good ways to let the public know what you are doing. Consider renting or asking for the mailing list from church or civic groups and do a special mailing about your event. The civic organization might simply let you include a copy of your publicity with their normal mailing.

12 Be prepared for a successful event that exceeds your expectations. Civic events that touch a positive, responsive chord in people have a life of their own. Unexpected good things happen. Be ready to ride the crest of the wave you have initiated, looking for all the ways you can piggyback on the success of your first event to continue your goals toward ending racism.

13 Follow up the event. Send thank-you notes to the speakers. Follow through on any suggestions made by the presenters or the audience. Make plans for your next event.

REFERENCES

Bobo, K., J. Kendall, and S. Max, op. cit.

40

Create
a Support Group

Develop a core group of like-minded individuals
within your community.

Bringing an end to racism takes many people work-
ing together from the personal to the global level. Contribute to this
shared task by creating a local support network of people interested
in ending racism. Developing a support network like this is very
easy. Start with two or three friends you know who share your
interests, and ask each of them to suggest two or three more individuals. You might resist the urge to make the group formal—deciding on a name, creating bylaws, electing officers. Trust that a group
of like-minded individuals has enough vitality to grow in its own
authentic way.

FUNCTIONS OF A SUPPORT GROUP

- *Consciousness-raising.* The group can learn more about racism and ways of ending it.
- *Process orientation.* The group can work within itself to ex-
  plore and change personal beliefs and attitudes toward racism.

- *Action orientation.* The group can pursue activities to bring an end to racism in the outside community.

STEPS YOU CAN TAKE

- Make sure members reflect the ethnic diversity of the community you live in.
- Use this book as a guide for your discussions and actions. Start at the beginning of this book and take at most five items from those sections entitled "Steps You Can Take." Discuss each item among the group. If the item calls for some action to be taken, determine how much of that action your group is ready for. Continue this until your group has covered each of the fifty items in this book.
- Invite outside speakers to address your group. Many institutions in your community have speakers ready to address your group about bringing an end to racism. Contact local civic organizations, political leaders, a local college or university, the local or state human resource agency, to find out who is available.
- Create a list of books related to ending racism. Choose a book a month to read and discuss among members of the group.
- Rent or watch an education videotape as a group.
- Learn and practice conflict resolution and intercultural communication skills.

41

Develop
a Community Vision
of Eliminating Racism

Create a vision of what ending racism means for
the community you live in.

Having a vision of ending racism in your commu-
nity is a first step toward realizing that goal. A vision statement for
your community will help identify what you feel is most important
in bringing an end to racism; it will highlight those areas where you
can direct your efforts; it will inspire others to work toward ending
racism; and it will be a source of personal strength for you to continue your work.

Like a personal vision statement, a community vision statement
can take many forms—an essay, a poem, a song, artwork, or some
other form of creative expression. It can be done on a large or small
scale. For example, the vision statement might be a community
mural of different ethnic groups living and working together in harmony. In the process of creating such a mural you would work with
many different aspects of your community. The final product and
each step in its creation would contribute toward ending racism in
your community.

A SAMPLE COMMUNITY VISION OF ENDING RACISM

I envision this community supporting the needs and aspirations of all residents regardless of skin color, ethnic heritage, or religious faith. Residents of this community have equal access to affordable shelter and food; children have the opportunity to receive an education that teaches them the dignity and worth of all people; our legal and justice systems treat all residents fairly and impartially; our community supports the growth and development of locally owned businesses by all our residents. Residents of this community are able to live free from harassment, threats, and violence because of their skin color or ethnic heritage. By ensuring these basic rights, our community is taking a step toward ending racism.

STEPS YOU CAN TAKE

- Create a community vision statement. See step 18 for suggestions on the form the vision statement might take.
- Consider a vision statement that might be on display at a prominent location in the community, like a mural or statue.
- Involve different organizations in the development of the vision statement. Contact local civic and social action groups to contribute ideas for the vision statement.
- Send a copy of the vision statement to the editor of the local newspaper for publication.
- Send copies of the vision statement to all local political, social, and business leaders.
- Post copies of the vision statement at prominent locations around the community.
- Obtain television time on a free local community-access cable network to present and discuss your community vision statement.
- Write a letter to the mayor suggesting the vision statement become part of an official proclamation on ending racism.

FOR THE NATION

42

Know Your Rights

Federal, state, and local laws have basic safeguards designed to protect citizens from racism.

The first ten amendments to the United States Constitution are known as the Bill of Rights (see the next section). They formally state the fundamental rights guaranteed to all citizens of this nation. Over the years additional amendments have been added to expand upon these fundamental rights with important implications for ending racism and oppression in this country (these amendments are also listed in the next section). When the Bill of Rights was drafted, for example, African Americans and Native Americans were not considered citizens and women did not have the right to vote. Subsequent amendments addressed situations like these: The Fifteenth Amendment, for example, granted African Americans and other minorities the right to vote.

Constitutional amendments are not the only basis of civil rights and legal protection from racism in this country. In the past thirty years federal, state, and local legislation has been enacted to ensure civil rights for all citizens. Often this legislation has overturned decades of racist laws like those forbidding interracial marriages and those requiring separate public facilities for African Americans. The

Civil Rights Act of 1964 was one major piece of legislation that sought to correct such abuses in America. In the late 1980s the Supreme Court under the Reagan administration overturned many civil rights cases based on this act and other civil rights legislation. The Civil Rights Act of 1991 reversed the losses of the Reagan era.

Laws, by themselves, will not bring an end to racism. Citizens who know their legal rights can help to end racism. Laws against racism provide legal remedies for victims and punishment for violators. Use the law to end racism: know your rights and take appropriate action when those rights are violated.

THE BILL OF RIGHTS

The First Ten Amendments to the U.S. Constitution

AMENDMENT I

Congress shall make no law respecting an establishment of religion, or prohibiting the free exercise thereof; or abridging the freedom of speech, or of the press; or the right of the people peaceably to assemble, and to petition the Government for a redress of grievances.

AMENDMENT II

A well-regulated Militia being necessary to the security of a free State, the right of the people to keep and bear Arms shall not be infringed.

AMENDMENT III

No soldier shall, in time of peace, be quartered in any house without the consent of the Owner; nor in time of war but in a manner to be prescribed by law.

AMENDMENT IV

The right of the people to be secure in their persons, houses, papers and effects, against unreasonable searches and seizures, shall not be violated, and no Warrants shall issue but upon probable cause, supported by Oath or affirmation, and particularly describing the place to be searched, and the persons or things to be seized.

AMENDMENT V

No person shall be held to answer for a capital or otherwise infamous crime, unless on a presentment or indictment of a Grand Jury, except in cases arising in the land or naval forces, or in the Militia, when in actual service in time of War or public danger; nor shall any person be subject for the same offense to be twice put in jeopardy of life or limb; nor shall be compelled in any criminal case to be a witness against himself, nor be deprived of life, liberty, or property, without due process of law; nor shall private property be taken for public use, without just compensation.

AMENDMENT VI

In all criminal prosecutions the accused shall enjoy the right to a speedy and public trial, by an impartial jury of the State and district wherein the crime shall have been committed, which district shall have been previously ascertained by law, and to be informed of the nature and cause of the accusation; to be confronted with the witnesses against him; to have compulsory process for obtaining witnesses in his favor, and to have the Assistance of Counsel for his defense.

AMENDMENT VII

In Suits at common law, where the value in controversy shall exceed twenty dollars, the right of trial by jury shall be preserved, and no fact tried by a jury shall be otherwise reexamined in any Court of the United States than according to the rules of the common law.

AMENDMENT VIII

Excessive bail shall not be required, nor excessive fines imposed, nor cruel and unusual punishments inflicted.

AMENDMENT IX

The enumeration in the Constitution of certain rights shall not be construed to deny or disparage others retained by the people.

AMENDMENT X

The powers not delegated to the United States by the Constitution, nor prohibited by it to the States, are reserved to the States respectively, or to the people.

OTHER CONSTITUTIONAL AMENDMENTS RELATED TO RACISM AND DISCRIMINATION

AMENDMENT XIII

SECTION 1.

Neither slavery nor involuntary servitude, except as a punishment for crime whereof the party shall have been duly convicted, shall exist within the United States, or any place subject to their jurisdiction.

AMENDMENT XIV

SECTION 1.

All persons born or naturalized in the United States, and subject to the jurisdiction thereof, are citizens of the United States and of the State wherein they reside. No State shall make or enforce any law which shall abridge the privileges or immunities of citizens of the United States; nor shall any State deprive any person of life, liberty, or property, without due process of law; nor deny to any person within its jurisdiction the equal protection of the laws.

SECTION 2.

Representatives shall be apportioned among the several States according to their respective numbers, counting the whole number of persons in each State, *excluding Indians not taxed.* But when the right to vote at any election for the choice of electors for President and Vice President of the United States, Representatives in Congress, the Executive and Judicial officers of a State, or the members of the Legislature thereof, is denied to any of the male inhabitants of such State, being twenty-one years of age, and citizens of the United States, or in any way abridged, except for participation in rebellion, or other crime, the basis of representation therein shall be reduced in the proportion which the number of such male citizens shall bear to the whole number of male citizens twenty-one years of age in such State.

SECTION 4.

The validity of the public debt of the United States, authorized by law, including debts incurred for payment of pensions and bounties for services in suppressing insurrection or rebellion, shall not be questioned. But neither the United States nor any State shall assume or pay any debt or obligation incurred in aid of insurrection or rebellion against the United States, or *any claim for the loss or emancipation of any slave;* but all such debts, obligations and claims shall be held illegal and void.

AMENDMENT XV
SECTION 1.

The right of citizens of the United States to vote shall not be denied or abridged by the United States or by any State on account of race, color, or previous condition of servitude.

AMENDMENT XIX

The right of citizens of the United States to vote shall not be denied or abridged by the United States or by any State on account of sex.

BASIC RIGHTS YOU SHOULD KNOW

Your Rights in Public Accommodations

This includes restaurants, amusement facilities, cemeteries, hotels, medical facilities, business establishments, public washrooms, public libraries, public schools, nursery and day care facilities, and pub-lic parks.

- Federal law prohibits discrimination on the basis of race, color, religion, national origin, or disability at any public facility.
- See step 29 for information about evaluating racism and dis-crimination in an institution.

Steps You Can Take If You Feel Your Rights Have Been Violated

- File a charge with the U.S. Department of Justice.
- File a charge with your state's human rights commission.
- File a charge with a local human rights agency (like the NAACP, the ACLU, or the Anti-Defamation League of B'nai B'rith).
- Seek legal help and file a lawsuit.

Your Rights in Education

- State laws provide for equal educational opportunities. Public schools may not discriminate against a student on the basis of economic status, race, color, sex, national origin, creed, or disability.
- Federal law provides for the separation of church and state. Public schools must guarantee students' rights to freedom of religion and provide instruction that is free from religious influ-ence.
- State and local laws may provide for choice in which schools students can attend. With some exceptions, students generally may elect to choose a school closest to their residence. Excep-tions apply in situations where desegregation is being forced, or special educational needs are being met.
- Contact your local school administration for more information regarding your educational rights as a citizen.

• See step 30 for information about eliminating racism in education.

Steps You Can Take If You Feel Your Rights Have Been Violated

• File a charge with your local school administrator.
• File a charge with your local board of education.
• File a charge with your state's department of education.
• File a charge with your state's human rights commission.
• File a charge with the U.S. Department of Justice.
• File a charge with a local human rights organization.
• Seek legal help and file a lawsuit.

Your Rights in Housing

• Federal law prohibits discrimination on the basis of race, color, religion, sex, national origin, or disability:
  • when buying or renting housing
  • in advertising for the rental or purchase of a home
  • in mortgage lending and home financing
  • in brokerage services
• Other discriminatory practices that are prohibited by many state and local laws are:
  • *Redlining,* the refusal of a bank to provide a mortgage for anyone within a certain geographic area.
  • *Blockbusting,* exploiting racial prejudice to lower the selling price of houses within an area.
  • *Steering,* showing homes based on the race, color, religion, or national origin of the buyer.
  • *Restrictive covenants,* a clause in a contract, for example, that prohibits the sale of property to members of a certain racial, religious, or ethnic group.
• See step 34 for more information on ending racism in housing.

Steps You Can Take If You Feel Your Rights Have Been Violated

- File a charge with the U.S. Department of Housing and Urban Development (HUD). Local offices can be found in your telephone book.
- File a charge with the human rights commission of your state.
- File a charge with a local human rights organization.
- Seek legal help and file a lawsuit.

Your Rights in Employment

- Your employer cannot discriminate against you on the basis of race, color, sex, age, religion, nationality, or disability in:
  - hiring, firing, promotion, or discipline
  - the conditions and terms of your employment when compared to other employees
  - harassing you, or allowing other employees to harass you
  - creating or allowing you to work in a hostile or offensive work environment (for example, you have a right to work where racist jokes are not told)
- See step 31 for additional information regarding ending racism in employment

Steps You Can Take If You Feel Your Rights Have Been Violated

- File a charge with the U.S. Equal Employment Opportunity Commission (EEOC).
- File a charge with the National Labor Relations Board (NLRB).
- File a charge with your state's human rights commission.
- File a charge with a local human rights agency.
- Seek legal advice and file a lawsuit.

RESOURCES

Office of Fair Housing and Equal Opportunity, Room 5116, De-
partment of Housing and Urban Development, 451 Seventh
Street, S.W., Washington, D.C. 20410. (202) 708-2878.
National Employment Lawyers Association, 535 Pacific Avenue,
San Francisco, CA 94133. (415) 397-6335. Lawyers specializ-
ing in employment discrimination.

43

Exercise
Your Right to Vote

A ballot is a powerful tool in ending racism.

The right to vote, though fundamental to a democracy, has long been used as a weapon against ethnic minorities. In the South after the Civil War, for example, racism flourished because former black slaves were denied the right to vote. Meanwhile, white Southerners voted to support political candidates who carried on a system of oppression and discrimination every bit as brutal as slavery.

With the passage of the Voting Rights Act in 1964 and the progress made by the civil rights movement, blacks began to exercise their right to vote and political change began to creep into rural and urban America. Blacks were elected mayors of large and small cities, and voted onto city councils; they were elected as state senators and representatives, and as congressional representatives.

Votes cannot change attitudes about racism, but they can change the laws that govern how people live. Votes can translate into laws that prohibit acts of racism and discrimination, and laws that promote equal treatment and equal opportunity for all ethnic groups. Votes can help change the face of our political institutions so they are more ethnically representative of the population they serve. Your vote is your voice; speak out with it.

STEPS YOU CAN TAKE

- Register to vote. Call your local voter registration office for locations where you can register. Your telephone book should list this number under "Government Offices." You can also call city hall, a local library, or the office of an elected representative to find out where and how you can register to vote.
- Learn how the election process for local, state, and national offices works in your state. For example, in national presidential elections states have different processes for selecting delegates for presidential candidates.
- Vote in every election: local, state, and national.
- Write or call candidates for written statements of their views about ending racism.
- Learn about the actual voting record of candidates on issues related to ending racism. See step 15 for information on using computer networks for this information. Also see step 28 for information on how to find out the views of local leaders.
- Volunteer for the election of candidates with good views and a good voting record on ending racism.
- Sign ballot initiatives and petitions that will help end racism. You need to be a registered voter to have your signature count on such documents.

ADDITIONAL RESOURCES

National Coalition on Black Voter Participation, 1629 K Street, NW, Suite 801, Washington, D.C. 20006. (202) 659-4929.
The League of Women Voters. For local branches check your yellow pages.

44

Join a National Organization Working to Eliminate Racism

There are many organizations working to end racism. Your membership will contribute to ongoing efforts.

Joining an organization founded to eliminate racism is a simple but important step. Membership is the lifeblood of any organization. Most organizations working to end racism have nominal membership fees that help with ongoing operating expenses. Your membership will be a financial contribution to the organization. It will also be a moral contribution, because your membership lets the organization know its goals are worthy of support. But don't let your effort end with the membership fee.

These organizations also look to their membership as a source of "people power" to get things done. The organization will usually have a list of standing committees you can participate on. Your voice and vote will count for something. You might find skills you never thought valuable to ending racism are needed by the organization—bookkeeping, driving a car, operating a computer, or making phone calls. Most organizations working to end racism are multiethnic and encourage membership from all ethnic groups.

STEPS YOU CAN TAKE

- First consider joining an organization that has a local chapter. This organization will have a history of working to eliminate racism in your community. If you live in a small community you'll probably know some of the other members already.
- Choose an organization as you would a friend. Go to a meeting, listen to what people are saying, ask questions, and select an organization that feels right to you.
- Make sure the organization is aware of all your skills, interests, and hobbies. You may be surprised by what is needed to help the organization.
- Consider joining an organization even if there is no local chapter. Write to the national headquarters about membership and also ask how you can help. The national or international headquarters will be very happy to let you know how you can help.
- Start a local chapter of an organization whose purpose is to eliminate racism. Many national organizations really need individuals to start a local chapter in smaller communities they do not ordinarily serve. The national headquarters will have all the information you need to start a local chapter.

ORGANIZATIONS WORKING TO END RACISM

Three of the Oldest

ACLU (American Civil Liberties Union) 132 West 43rd Street, New York, NY 10036, (212) 944-9800. By charter the ACLU is not affiliated with any particular ethnic group. The goal of this organization is to work against the abuses of government that violate the civil rights and liberties of all citizens.

ADL (Anti-Defamation League of B'nai B'rith) 823 United Nations Plaza, New York, NY 10017, (212) 490-2525. The ADL was formed in 1913 to battle anti-Semitism in the United States. Over the years the ADL's mission has expanded to confront bigotry and racism of all forms.

NAACP (National Association for the Advancement of Colored People) 4805 Mt. Hope Drive, Baltimore, MD 21215, (410) 358-8900. Founded in 1909, and one of the oldest civil rights organizations in America, the NAACP has been in the forefront of fighting for voting rights, job discrimination, desegregation, and civil rights. Membership in the NAACP is open to members of all ethnic groups.

Other National Organizations Working to End Racism

National Alliance Against Racist and Political Repression (NAARPR), 11 John Street, Room 202, New York, NY 10038. (212) 406-3330.

Center for Constitutional Rights (formerly Civil Rights Legal Defense Fund), 666 Broadway, 7th Floor, New York, NY 10012. (212) 614-6464.

Leadership Conference on Civil Rights, 1629 K Street, NW, Suite 1010, Washington, D.C. 20006. (202) 466-3311.

SCLC (Southern Christian Leadership Conference), 334 Auburn Avenue, NE, Atlanta, GA 30312. (404) 522-1420.

Southern Poverty Law Center, Box 2087, Montgomery, AL 36102. (205) 264-0286.

A. Philip Randolph Institute, 1444 I Street, NW, Suite 300, Washington, D.C. 20005. (202) 289-2774.

National Urban League (NUL), 500 E. 62nd St., New York, NY 10021. (212) 310-9000.

ADC (American-Arab Anti-Discrimination Committee) 4201 Connecticut Avenue, NW, Suite 500, Washington, D.C. 20008. (202) 244-2990.

Asian-American Legal Defense and Education Fund, 99 Hudson Street, New York, NY 10013. (212) 966-5932.

Chinese for Affirmative Action, 17 Walter U. Lum Place, San Francisco, CA 94108. (415) 274-6750.

CORE (Congress of Racial Equality), 30 Cooper Square, New York, NY 10003. (212) 598-4000.

Klanwatch Project of the Southern Poverty Law Center, 400 Washington Street, Montgomery, AL 36101. (205) 264-0286.

LULAC (League of United Latin American Citizens), 1600 E. Desert Inn Road, Suite 204A, Las Vegas, NV 89109. (702) 792-8160.

NAACP Legal Defense and Education Fund, 99 Hudson Street, New York, NY 10013. (212) 219-1900.

National Institute Against Prejudice and Violence, 712 West Lombard Street, Baltimore, MD 21201. (410) 706-5170.

National Jewish Community Relations Advisory Council, 443 Park Avenue South, New York, NY 10016. (212) 684-6950.

People for the American Way, 2000 M Street NW, Suite 400, Washington, D.C. 20036. (202) 467-4999.

Puerto Rican Legal Defense and Education Fund, 99 Hudson Street, New York, NY 10013. (212) 219-3360.

45

Let National Leaders Know Your Views

Political leaders thrive on the views and opinions of their constituency.

Political leaders are very sensitive to the views and opinions of the people who vote them into office. You can make your vote count beyond Election Day by letting your elected representatives know your views on issues related to racism. Political leaders can get "out of touch" with the sentiments of their constituency. Some leaders hold local forums or town meetings to learn about citizens' needs and beliefs. There are many ways and opportunities for you to contact elected officials and let them know how you think they can better help to eliminate racism. Communicating with elected representatives in this way is one of the rights and responsibilities of citizens living in a democracy. Your voice, like your vote, can make a difference.

STEPS YOU CAN TAKE

- Keep the names, addresses, and telephone numbers of your elected representatives handy.
- Call or write your national elected representatives to let them

know your feelings about local, national, or global issues and events related to ending racism. Chances are you won't speak directly to the elected representative—you may get a recording, or an administrative assistant. Speak or write clearly and simply, expressing your views in the fewest possible words. You may also choose to use a postcard, letter, fax, telegram, or computer-generated letter (see step 15).

- Enlist the support of like-minded individuals and send your representatives a letter signed by many people about an issue or event related to ending racism. You might also publish that letter in a local newspaper.
- Contact your representatives in response to a vote they are about to take, or may have already taken, on issues related to ending racism. For example, if a civil-rights bill is pending, call your congressional representatives and let them know it's important to you that they vote in favor of the bill.
- When your elected representatives come home to campaign for reelection, visit their offices. Make an appointment to see them and personally express your feelings about steps they might take to end racism.
- Attend town-hall meetings or local forums organized by elected officials and speak out about the importance of taking steps to end racism.
- Enlist the support of national representatives in local projects to eliminate racism. If you've planned a multicultural food festival, a spiritual unity day, or other local event, contact your national representatives and ask for their support. You may get a proclamation from their offices that you can read at the event or publish in the local newspaper. You might even get their attendance. At the very least their stand on ending racism will be a matter of public record.

RESOURCES

Local officials, voting registration office, mayor's office, county executive's office or public library for names, addresses, and telephone numbers of congressional representatives.

46

Develop a National Vision of Eliminating Racism

Create a vision of the importance of ending racism nationally.

A democracy is designed to give voice to the legitimate concerns of all its citizens. Developing a national vision statement will help you articulate your concerns about ending racism; raise those concerns with the appropriate leaders; and support your efforts to bring an end to racism. National political leaders—senators and representatives—listen to the opinions of their constituencies "back home." A national vision statement is a way of expressing the attitudes and beliefs you would like your elected representatives to reflect in the legislation they create and the policies they enforce.

Like the personal vision statement, the national vision statement can take any number of forms—a letter, a prayer, a song, a poem, or some other creative expression. If you intend for this statement to be sent to elected representatives, be aware they are most accustomed to responding to written letters. Developing a national vision statement is small step you can take that may result in many larger steps being taken to end racism.

A SAMPLE NATIONAL VISION OF ENDING RACISM

This country has the ability to ensure that rights defined in the Constitution, the Bill of Rights, and other great national documents are extended to all citizens regardless of their skin color or ethnic background. Our national institutions play a crucial role in helping to end racism and discrimination, and ensure the rights of all citizens. The Senate and House of Representatives must continue to create and support legislation outlawing racism in all forms and at all levels in this country. The judicial system must uphold the laws that have contributed toward ending racism, and provided equal opportunity for those who have been hurt by years of racism and discrimination. And the executive branch of government must provide the moral and political leadership to guide this country toward the elimination of racism.

I believe this country must honor, respect, and treasure its most valuable national resource—its people, who are of all different colors and come from all different ethnic backgrounds. Bringing an end to racism and discrimination is an important step in protecting this national human treasure.

STEPS YOU CAN TAKE

- Create a national vision statement. See step 18 for suggestions about the form of this statement.
- Enlist the aid of other groups or interested people in developing the national vision statement.
- Develop the vision statement as a letter upon which you can obtain signatures. Create a local and/or national campaign to obtain signatures to the letter.
- Organize an effort to publish this letter with the signatures of like-minded individuals in a national newspaper *(The New York Times, The Wall Street Journal, The Washington Post).*
- Send copies of the letter to your congressional representatives.

Include the letter along with a request for them to act on a particular piece of pending legislation that would help to eliminate racism. Expect a form letter acknowledging your statement.

- Send a copy to the President of the United States. Include with the letter a request for him/her to take action on a national measure that would bring an end to racism.

FOR THE WORLD

47

Support Global Efforts to Affirm Human Rights

Human rights will not be protected if left solely to the governments of this world. . . .
Important as bills and rights and legal mechanisms are, still more important is the concern of one individual for another, one group for another, one nation for another.

—Mumtaz Soysal
Former Turkish Prisoner of Conscience

Racism occurs everywhere: in South Africa, the Balkans, the Middle East, Germany, England, America, throughout the world. And it goes by different names: *apartheid, ethnic cleansing, xenophobia, anti-Semitism, white supremacy, discrimination, segregation.* Yet regardless of where it occurs, or what it is called, racism denies people fundamental human rights. As a violation of human rights, racism has been outlawed by conventions of the United Nations as a crime against humanity—though the organization itself lacks the power to enforce such conventions.

In the absence of international enforcement authority, concerned people throughout the world have mounted efforts to secure and protect human rights. Ending racism is part of this effort. Working through governmental organizations (called GOs) like the United Nations and nongovernmental organizations (called NGOs) like Amnesty International and Helsinki Watch, human rights advocates have taken action in a number of areas: (1) as watchdogs, monitoring human rights abuses; (2) documenting and reporting the facts of human rights abuses; (3) organizing campaigns to protest abuses of human rights; (4) crafting international legislation to promote and secure human rights; (5) encouraging public educational drives in support of human rights; and (6) promoting the very rare use of force by one or more governments to protect and defend human rights.

THINK GLOBALLY, ACT LOCALLY

"Where, after all, do universal human rights begin?" United Nations founding member Eleanor Roosevelt asked rhetorically in a 1958 address. She answered by noting that human rights begin in our communities, our schools, our farms, our factories, and our offices. "Unless these rights have meaning there, they have little meaning anywhere. Without concerned citizen action to uphold them close to home, we shall look in vain for progress in the larger world."

Our individual actions to end racism do have meaning and purpose far outside our individual world. For our individual world is composed of others who have individual worlds composed of others, and so on, in an unbroken, interdependent chain that spans humanity and the globe. As the Berlin Wall fell in 1990 the voices of concerned German citizens could be heard singing "We Shall Overcome," a song that originated in the freedom movement of African Americans. And as Chinese students in Tienanmen Square bravely stood up for freedom and justice, they could also be heard singing "We Shall Overcome." One could not help hearing, in these words sung around the world, the simple refusal of Rosa Parks to move to the back of a Birmingham bus in 1955. Her individual action gave birth to a movement for civil and human rights that is continually being reborn throughout the world. One person *can* make a difference.

DID YOU KNOW . . .

- Article 1 of the charter of the United Nations, adopted in 1945, states that one major purpose of the United Nations is to "achieve international cooperation in solving international problems of an economic, social, cultural, or humanitarian character, and in promoting and encouraging respect for human rights and for fundamental freedoms for all without distinction as to race, sex, language, or religion. . . ."
- The Universal Declaration of Human Rights was adopted by the United Nations in 1948 (see the appendix of selections from this document).
- An international convention against slavery was adopted by the UN in 1949.
- An international convention against discrimination in employment and occupation was adopted by the UN in 1958.
- An international convention against discrimination in education was adopted by the UN in 1960.
- The United Nations Declaration on the Elimination of All Forms of Racial Discrimination was adopted in 1963.
- The International Convention on the Elimination of All Forms of Racial Discrimination was adopted in 1965.
- The Helsinki Agreement signed at the conclusion of the 1975 Conference on Security and Cooperation in Europe stated, "The participating States recognize the universal significance of human rights and fundamental freedoms, respect for which is an essential factor for the peace, justice, and well-being necessary to ensure the development of friendly relations and cooperation among themselves as among all States."
- Disenchantment by NGOs and other groups working on behalf of human rights with the United Nations' efforts in human rights comes, in part, from unwritten diplomatic protocols protecting member nations from explicit identification as human rights violators; and by UN censuring of NGOs that pointed to failures of the organization to act on cases of gross human rights violations.

- The United States has signed but not ratified the following international human rights conventions adopted by the United Nations:

  The International Convention on Civil and Political Rights
  The International Convention on Economic, Social, and
    Civil Rights
  The Convention Against Torture and other Cruel, Inhuman,
    or Degrading Treatment or Punishment

STEPS YOU CAN TAKE

- Join an international organization working to eliminate racism and bring about universal human rights.
- Send for copies of the annual reports issues by human rights watchdog groups like Amnesty International and Helsinki Watch.
- Respond to an Urgent Action (UA) appeal issued by Amnesty International (AI). UAs are issued by AI on behalf of individuals or groups who are in imminent danger—political prisoners undergoing torture, groups brutalized by police, protesters being hunted by authorities. Each UA consists of: (1) a report of all known facts of the case; (2) background information about the case; (3) a call for support in the form of letters, faxes, telegrams; and (4) detailed information (names, addresses, telephone and fax numbers) on how to respond to the UA. If you have a personal computer (see step 15) you can receive this information over a network such as CompuServe, and you can respond back with a fax over the same network.
- Adopt a prisoner of conscience and work on behalf of his or her relief. Contact any of the human rights organizations listed in this book for information about this kind of program.
- Become a local human-rights watchdog. Look around your community for instances of human rights violations. Many of the suggestions in other sections of this book will help you do this.

- Start a local group involved with protecting and securing human rights.
- Become a resource person on human rights. Write to human rights organizations for literature, clip newspaper articles about human rights, study the issues and become informed.
- Disseminate information on human rights in your community. Ask your local library, bookstore, and educational institutions to carry educational and information materials on human rights—books, films, audiotapes, brochures.
- Let local, state, and national elected leaders know your views. Stay in touch with U.S. foreign policy regarding human rights, then write your representatives and senators. Express your thoughts and feelings about how well the U.S. is living up to its obligations to protect human rights domestically and internationally; write about the government's position on ratifying international conventions and covenants on human rights.

REFERENCES

Amnesty International. *The Amnesty International Handbook.* Alameda, CA: Hunter House, Inc., 1992.

Meltzer, Milton. *The Human Rights Book.* New York: McGraw-Hill Publishing Co., 1979. The quotes in this section from Eleanor Roosevelt and Mumtaz Soysal are taken from this book.

Sherwin, Jane. *Human Rights.* Vero Beach, FL: Rourke Corp., 1990.

Sinetar, Marsha. *Human Rights for Children.* Alameda, CA: Hunter House, Inc., 1992.

Zimmerman, Richard, *What Can I Do to Make a Difference?: A Positive Action Sourcebook.* New York: Penguin Books, 1991.

Human Rights Organizations (Located in United States)

American Association for the International Commission of Jurists, 777 UN Plaza Suite 9E, New York, NY 10017. (212) 972-0883.

Amnesty International USA (AIUSA), 322 8th Avenue, New York, NY 10001. (212) 807-8400. AI has headquarters around the world.

Americas Watch, 485 5th Avenue, New York, NY 10017. (212) 972-8400.

Asia Watch Committee, 1522 K St., NW, Suite 910, Washington, D.C. 20005. (202) 371-6592.

Humanitas International, Box 818, Menlo Park, CA 94026.

Human Rights Associates, International, 341 Madison Avenue, Twentieth Floor, New York, NY 10017. (212) 986-5555.

Human Rights Campaign Fund, 1012 14th Street, NW, No. 607, Washington, D.C. 20005. (202) 628-4160.

Helsinki Watch, 485 5th Avenue, New York, NY 10017. (212) 972-8400.

Human Rights Watch, 485 5th Avenue, New York, NY 10017. (212) 972-8400.

International League for Human Rights, 432 Park Avenue South, Room 1103, New York, NY 10016. (212) 684-1221.

Middle East Watch, 485 5th Avenue, New York, NY 10017. (212) 972-8400.

Human Rights Organizations (International)

International Commission of Jurists, 26 Chemin de Joinville, boîte 160, CH-1216 Geneva, Switzerland. Tel. 22 788-4747.

United Nations Centre for Human Rights (Centre pour les Droits de l'Homme), Palais des Nations, CH-1211 Geneva, 10, Switzerland. Tel. 22 917-1234.

Amnesty International, 1 Easton Street, London WC1X-8DJ, England. Tel. 071-413-5500.

INTERNET, c/o Human Rights Center, University of Ottawa, 57 Louis Pasteur, Ottawa, ON, Canada K1N 6N5. (613) 564-3492.

Organizations Working to End Racism
(International)

International Organization for the Elimination of All Forms of Racial Discrimination, 41 rue de Zurich, CH-1201 Geneva, Switzerland. Tel. 22 731-5534.

Committee on the Elimination of Racial Discrimination, United Nations Centre for Human Rights, Palais des Nations, CH-1211
Geneva 10, Switzerland. Tel. 22 917-1234.

S.O.S. Racisme, 64 rue de la folie Mericourt, F-75011 Paris,
France. Tel. 1 480 6400.

TransAfrica, 545 8th Street, SE, Suite 200, Washington, D.C.
20003. (202) 547-2550.

Note: *When calling international telephone numbers check
with your overseas operator for dialing instructions.*

48

The Healing of Persons, Nations, and the World

Eliminating racism is intimately linked to other efforts aimed at personal, social, and global transformation.

Eliminating racism is not an isolated issue confined to the boundaries of a given nation. Racism is symptomatic of a blindness to the fundamental interconnectedness of all life. Racism sees difference without seeing harmony; separation without seeing wholeness; alienation without seeing communion; independence without seeing interdependence. This lack of vision gives rise to personal illness: we are alienated from ourselves. We have cut off our bodies from our minds. As a result our physical and mental health have suffered as we have become victims of the stress-related diseases of modern life.

This lack of vision gives rise to social illness. Racism is just one social disease that is based on fragmentation and separation. Sexism, violence against gays and lesbians, domestic violence, homelessness, and poverty are other social ills that spring from this same soil of separation and difference. And this lack of vision also gives rise to global illness. Independence, rather than interdependence, pits nation against nation, ethnic group against ethnic group, and religion against religion throughout the world. Moreover, this lack of global vision literally separates us from the planet we inhabit. The earth is oppressed by humankind in much the same way as one ethnic group is oppressed by another.

Eliminating racism is about healing the wounds of separation and fragmentation; of regaining our vision—personally, nationally, and globally. Eliminating racism is part of establishing a new ecology of the planet; an ecology that links what takes place within each human being to what takes place among human beings, and ultimately to what takes place between all species that inhabit the earth and the planet itself. The efforts put forth to eliminate racism contribute to other efforts at personal, social, and global transformation. For they are all aimed at ensuring the survival of humankind and the planet upon which we live.

STEPS YOU CAN TAKE

- Learn about and promote personal health and well-being—diet, exercise, stress reduction, emotional health, personal and spiritual growth.
- Learn about and contribute to ongoing efforts to address national issues like sexism, gay rights, animal rights, domestic violence, homelessness, and poverty.
- Learn about and contribute to ongoing efforts to address national issues and global issues related to racism—world hunger, environmental concerns, human rights, and world peace.
- Educate others about the interrelationship between racism and the healing of persons, nations, and the earth.
- Plan a joint public activity between an organization working on issues of personal, national, or global healing, and an organization working to eliminate racism. Examples: a forum on environmental racism; a workshop on stress reduction and racism; a presentation on sexism and racism.

CONCERNING THE ENVIRONMENT, DID YOU KNOW . . .

- 3 out of every 5 African and Hispanic Americans live in a neighborhood with a hazardous waste site.
- In Houston, Texas, with a 25% population of African Americans, 100% of the landfills and 75% of the garbage incinerators are located in black neighborhoods.
- One of the nation's largest landfills, housing waste from all of the eastern United States, is located in Emelle, Alabama, with a population that is 79% African American.
- Taking all other factors into consideration, race is the most significant variable that differentiates those communities with hazardous waste sites from those without.

REFERENCES

Bear, Sun, and Wabun Wind. *Black Dawn/Bright Day.* Spokane, WA: Bear Tribe Publishing, 1990.

Petrash, Carol A. *Earthways: Simple Environmental Activities for Young Children.* Mt. Rainier, MD: Gryphon House, Inc., 1992.

Rees, Mathew. "Black and Green: Race and Environmentalism." *The New Republic* (March 2, 1992).

Steinhart, P. "What Can We Do About Environmental Racism." *Audubon,* Vol. 93, No. 3 (May 1991).

The Earthworks Group. *Fifty Simple Things You Can Do to Save the Earth.* Berkeley, CA: Earthworks Press, 1989.

Wild, Russell, ed. *The Earth Care Annual.* Emmaus, PA: Rodale Press, Inc., published each year.

Zimmerman, Richard, op. cit.

RESOURCES

National Wildlife Federation, 1400 16th Street, NW, Washington, D.C. 20036. (202) 797-6800.

Native Americans for a Clean Environment, Box 1671, Tahlequah, OK 74465. (918) 458-4322.

Natural Resources Defense Council, 40 West 20th Street, New York, NY 10168. (212) 727-2700.

Sierra Club, 730 Polk Street, San Francisco, CA 94109. (415) 923-5660.

United Church of Christ Commission for Racial Justice, 700 Prospect Avenue E., Seventh Floor, Cleveland, OH 44115. (216) 736-2168. Rev. Benjamin Chavis, Jr., of the UCC, now head of the NAACP, chaired the first published study of environmental racism.

49

Develop a
Global Vision
of Eliminating Racism

There is no phenomenon in the universe that
does not intimately concern us, from a pebble
resting at the bottom of the ocean, to the
movement of a galaxy millions of light years away.

—Thich Nhat Hanh,
Vietnamese Scholar-Monk

In this vision statement you describe your feelings
about the global significance of ending racism and honoring diversity. A global vision statement can be an extension of the personal,
family, community, and national vision statements described in previous steps. It can also stand alone. As with the other vision statements, this global statement is a tool of empowerment, helping you
find a larger context for the individual actions you take. Like the
other vision statements, this global statement can take many forms:
an affirmation, a prayer, a poem, a song, a painting, a ritual, or any
other form of creative expression.

DECLARATION OF INTERDEPENDENCE

In 1975 the American historian Henry Steele Commager drafted a
Declaration of Interdependence:

We hold these truths to be self-evident: that all [people] are
created equal; that the inequalities and injustices which afflict

so much of the human race are the product of history and society, not God or nature; that people everywhere are entitled to the blessings of life and liberty, peace and security, and the realization of their full potential; that they have an inescapable moral obligation to preserve those rights for posterity; and that to achieve these ends all the peoples and nations of the world should acknowledge their interdependence and join together to dedicate their hearts to the solutions of those problems which threaten their survival.

A SAMPLE GLOBAL VISION STATEMENT

We live in an interconnected world. What happens in the world affects me. Wherever racism, intolerance, and ethnic strife exist, I am affected, whether it is in South Africa or South Los Angeles; Eastern Europe or the Middle East; a main street in urban America or a back road in rural America. Racism tears at the fabric of my connectedness with all humankind; it denies the fundamental wholeness of all people; and it ignores the bounty of diversity within the human family.

I express my belief in the worth and dignity of all people through my efforts to end racism and honor human diversity. Where I live, work, and play is a microcosm of the world. The actions I take toward ending racism—personally, in my family, in my community, and in my nation—not only affect this microcosm but contribute to worldwide efforts to accomplish similar ends. As more people join this effort to end racism and celebrate diversity, the world will be a more joyful place for all people to live in.

STEPS YOU CAN TAKE

- Set aside some time to develop a global vision statement (see step 18 for additional suggestions about creating a vision statement).
- Collect the quotes of world leaders and writers from around the

world about ending racism and honoring diversity. A librarian
could help you with this. Make a montage of these statements.
- Create a photomontage of people around the world of different colors, ways of life, and faiths. Use a magazine like *Life* or
National Geographic.
- Read the preamble to the universal declaration of human
rights, below, and have your global vision statement reflect
your feelings about that document.
- Place your global vision statement in some prominent location
(a refrigerator door, bathroom mirror, et cetera).
- Take time to read the statement.
- Change your vision statement as you learn more about the
global efforts to end racism and honor diversity.

UNIVERSAL DECLARATION OF HUMAN RIGHTS

Preamble

Whereas recognition of the inherent dignity and of the equal and
inalienable rights of all members of the human family is the foundation of freedom, justice, and peace in the world,

Whereas disregard and contempt for human rights have resulted
in barbarous acts which have outraged the conscience of mankind,
and the advent of a world in which human beings shall enjoy freedom of speech and belief and freedom from fear and want has been
proclaimed as the highest aspiration of the common people,

Whereas it is essential, if man is not to be compelled to have
recourse, as a last resort, to rebellion against tyranny and oppression, that human rights should be protected by the rule of law,

Whereas it is essential to promote the development of friendly
relations between nations,

Whereas the peoples of the United Nations have in the Charter
reaffirmed their faith in fundamental human rights, in the dignity
and worth of the human person, and in the equal rights of men and

women and have determined to promote social progress and better standards of life in larger freedom,

Whereas Member States have pledged themselves to achieve, in cooperation with the United Nations, the promotion of universal respect for and observance of human rights and fundamental freedoms,

Whereas a common understanding of these rights and freedoms is of the greatest importance for the full realization of this pledge,

Now, therefore,

The General Assembly

Proclaims this Universal Declaration of Human Rights as a common standard of achievement for all peoples and all nations, to the end that every individual and every organ of society, keeping this Declaration constantly in mind, shall strive by teaching and education to promote respect for these rights and freedoms and by progressive measures, national and international, to secure their universal and effective recognition and observance, both among the peoples of Member States themselves and among the peoples of territories under their jurisdiction.

United Nations
December 10, 1948

50

Become
a Messenger of Hope

Share your dreams, visions, and ideas about
ending racism and celebrating diversity with
someone else.

If you have come to the last step in this book, then
you have already taken a first step toward ending racism. Along the
way the ideas, suggestions, thoughts, and resources presented may
have kindled your inspiration. Stoke the fire, let the flames burn
bright. Follow your inspiration, wherever it leads—to further reading or research; to introspection and personal growth; to developing plans and taking actions. Become a messenger of hope: share
your inspiration with someone else. You can make a difference.
You can take another step toward ending racism by talking with
your family, friends, and neighbors, or by simply passing this book
along to them.

The fifty steps in this book can certainly be expanded and elabo-
rated upon. Perhaps you feel there are other important steps as
well. Write them down. Use an action-oriented format: label the
step, have a brief discussion, itemize the concrete actions someone
can take, prepare a list of references and resources. Let this description become the basis for personal action; share it with someone else. And please write us with your thoughts, ideas, visions, and

inspiration about the steps we can all take to eliminate racism and celebrate the diversity of our human family. Together let's spread a message of hope; let's spread the word that "We *Can* All Get Along." **WRITE TO:**

We *Can* All Get Along
P.O. Box 3056
Bellingham, WA 98227
TEL (206) 398-9355 FAX (206) 398-7631
CompuServe ID# 71426,72

About the Author
Clyde W. Ford

Clyde W. Ford was born in New York City and graduated from Wesleyan University in Middletown, Connecticut. He worked as a computer engineer with the IBM corporation, then left to pursue a career in chiropractic medicine. Dr. Ford is a graduate of the Psychosynthesis Institute of New York and Western States Chiropractic College.

Dr. Ford's undergraduate major was African American History. Toward completion of that degree he received the Danforth Research fellowship from Wesleyan University. While at Wesleyan University, Clyde also participated in the formation of the Institute of the Black World, an arm of the Martin Luther King, Jr., Memorial Center in Atlanta. He was among the first six students to attend that institute. Dr. Ford is a founding member of the Northern Puget Sound branch of the National Association for the Advancement of Colored People (NAACP) and currently serves as its press secretary and a member of the executive board. Clyde teaches a course on the African American experience at Western Washington University in Bellingham, Washington, and is also a member of the Presidential Advisory Committee on Minority Affairs at the university. Dr. Ford is the author of two previous books. Presently Dr. Ford writes, lectures widely, and maintains a private practice in Bellingham, Washington.